The Maryland Attorneys' Rules of Professional Conduct

Compliments of the Maryland State Bar Association, Inc.

2024

(Reprinted from Maryland Rules Annotated and updated with amendments through January 1, 2024)

AF759001

MSBA
MARYLAND STATE BAR ASSOCIATION

Maryland State Bar Association
520 W. Fayette Street
Baltimore, MD 21201
Main 410-685-7878
Toll free 800-492-1964
www.msba.org

The MSBA's publications and programs are intended to provide current and accurate information about subject matter covered and are designed to help attorneys maintain their professional competence. Publications are distributed and oral programs presented with the understanding that the MSBA does not render any legal, accounting, or other professional advice. Attorneys using MSBA publications or orally conveyed information in dealing with a specific client's (or their own) legal matters should also research original sources of authority.

Thurgood Marshall State Law Library Cataloging-in-Publication Data

Name: Maryland. Supreme Court.
Title: Maryland attorneys' rules of professional conduct.
Description: Baltimore, Md. : MSBA, 2024.
Subjects: Legal ethics—Maryland.
Other name: Maryland State Bar Association.
Classification: LCC KFM1276.5.A2 A3 2024

ISBN 978-1-960444-43-1

Table of Contents

COUNSELOR

ADVOCATE

TRANSACTIONS WITH PERSONS OTHER THAN CLIENTS

FIRMS AND ASSOCIATIONS

PUBLIC SERVICE

INFORMATION ABOUT LEGAL SERVICES

MAINTAINING THE INTEGRITY OF THE PROFESSION

IDEALS OF PROFESSIONALISM

GUIDELINES OF ADVOCACY FOR ATTORNEYS REPRESENTING CHILDREN IN CINA AND RELATED TPR AND ADOPTION PROCEEDINGS

STATEMENT OF THE ISSUE

Foreword

The Maryland State Bar Association, Inc. (MSBA) is pleased to present to attorneys newly admitted to the Maryland bar this complimentary copy of the *Maryland Attorneys' Rules of Professional Conduct and Attorney Trust Accounts*.

This edition is fully up to date with all amendments received through January 1, 2024.

The MSBA Publications and Content Department offers over 200 publications in the form of practice manuals, handbooks, program materials, and forms. MSBA's publications address more than 20 discrete areas of law practice, utilizing a volunteer corps of hundreds of experienced and respected practitioners, judges and professionals. Please visit our online catalog at https://www.msba.org/site/content/News-and-Publications/Treatises-and-Coursebooks.aspx for additional publication information.

We actively solicit your comments and suggestions. If you believe that there are additional rules, or statutes which should be included (or excluded), please write to us or call us 1-410-685- 7878 or toll-free at 1-800-492-1964; fax us at 410-685-1016; or E-mail us at msba@msba.org. By providing your informed comments, you will be assured of having available a working tool which increases in value each year.

January 2024

The Maryland Attorneys' Rules of Professional Conduct and Attorney Trusts Accounts

PUBLIC SERVICE

INFORMATION ABOUT LEGAL SERVICES

MAINTAINING THE INTEGRITY OF THE PROFESSION

THE MARYLAND ATTORNEYS' RULES OF PROFESSIONAL CONDUCT

Preamble: An Attorney's Responsibilities

[1] An attorney, as a member of the legal profession, is a representative of clients, an officer of the legal system and a public citizen having special responsibility for the quality of justice.

[2] As a representative of clients, an attorney performs various functions. As advisor, an attorney provides a client with an informed understanding of the client's legal rights and obligations and explains their practical implications. As advocate, an attorney zealously asserts the client's position under the rules of the adversary system. As negotiator, an attorney seeks a result advantageous to the client but consistent with requirements of honest dealing with others. As evaluator, an attorney acts by examining a client's legal affairs and reporting about them to the client or to others.

[3] In addition to these representational functions, an attorney may serve as a third-party neutral, a nonrepresentational role helping the parties to resolve a dispute or other matter. Some of these Rules apply directly to attorneys who are or have served as third-party neutrals. See, e.g., Rules 19–301.12 and 19–302.4 (1.12 and 2.4). In addition, there are Rules that apply to attorneys who are not active in the practice of law or to practicing attorneys even when they are acting in a nonprofessional capacity. For example, an attorney who commits fraud in the conduct of a business is subject to discipline for engaging in conduct involving dishonesty, fraud, deceit or misrepresentation. See Rule 19–308.4 (8.4).

[4] In all professional functions an attorney should be competent, prompt and diligent. An attorney should maintain communication with a client concerning the representation. An attorney should keep in confidence information relating to representation of a client except so far as disclosure is required or permitted by the Maryland Attorneys' Rules of Professional Conduct or other law.

[5] An attorney's conduct should conform to the requirements of the law, both in professional service to clients and in the attorney's business and personal affairs. An attorney should use the law's procedures only for legitimate purposes and not to harass or intimidate others. An attorney should demonstrate respect for the legal system and for those who serve it, including judges, other attorneys and public officials. While it is an attorney's duty, when necessary, to challenge the rectitude of official action, it is also an attorney's duty to uphold legal process.

[6] As a public citizen, an attorney should seek improvement of the law, access to the legal system, the administration of justice and the quality of service rendered by the legal profession. As a member of a learned profession, an attorney should cultivate knowledge of the law beyond its use for clients, employ that knowledge in reform of the law and work to strengthen legal education. In addition, an attorney should further the public's understanding of and confidence in the rule of law and the justice system because legal institutions in a constitutional democracy depend on popular participation and support to maintain their authority. An attorney should be mindful of deficiencies in the administration of justice and of the fact that the poor, and sometimes persons who are not poor, cannot afford adequate legal assistance. Therefore, all attorneys should devote professional time and resources and use civic influence to ensure equal access to our system of justice for all those who because of economic or social barriers cannot afford or secure adequate legal advice or representation. An attorney should aid the legal profession in pursuing these objectives and should help the bar regulate itself in the public interest.

[7] Many of an attorney's professional responsibilities are prescribed in the Maryland Attorneys' Rules of Professional Conduct, as well as substantive and procedural law. However, an attorney is also guided by personal conscience and the approbation of professional peers. An attorney should strive to attain the highest level of skill, to improve the law and the legal profession and to exemplify the legal profession's ideals of public service.

[8] An attorney's responsibilities as a representative of clients, an officer of the legal system and a public citizen are usually harmonious. Thus, when an opposing party is well represented, an attorney can be a zealous advocate on behalf of a client and at the same time assume that justice is being done. So also, an attorney can be sure that preserving client confidences ordinarily serves the public interest because people are more likely to seek legal advice, and thereby heed their legal obligations, when they know their communications will be private.

[9] In the nature of law practice, however, conflicting responsibilities are encountered. Virtually all difficult ethical problems arise from conflict between an attorney's responsibilities to clients, to the legal system and to the attorney's own interest in remaining an ethical individual while earning a satisfactory living. The Maryland Attorneys' Rules of Professional Conduct often prescribe terms for resolving such conflicts. Within the framework of these Rules, however, many difficult issues of professional discretion can arise. Such issues must be resolved through the exercise of sensitive professional and moral judgment guided by the basic principles underlying the Rules. These principles include the attorney's obligation zealously to protect and pursue a client's legitimate interests, within the bounds of the law, while maintaining a professional, courteous and civil attitude toward all persons involved in the legal system.

[10] The legal profession is largely self-governing. Although other professions also have been granted powers of self- government, the legal profession is unique in this respect because of the close relationship between the profession and the processes of government and law enforcement. This connection is manifested in the fact that ultimate authority over the legal profession is vested largely in the courts.

[11] To the extent that attorneys meet the obligations of their professional calling, the occasion for government regulation is obviated. Self-regulation also helps maintain the legal profession's independence from government domination. An independent legal

profession is an important force in preserving government under law, for abuse of legal authority is more readily challenged by a profession whose members are not dependent on government for the right to practice.

[12] The legal profession's relative autonomy carries with it special responsibilities of self-government. The profession has a responsibility to assure that its regulations are conceived in the public interest and not in furtherance of parochial or self- interested concerns of the bar. Every attorney is responsible for observance of the Maryland Attorneys' Rules of Professional Conduct. An attorney should also aid in securing their observance by other attorneys. Neglect of these responsibilities compromises the independence of the profession and the public interest which it serves.

[13] Attorneys play a vital role in the preservation of society. The fulfillment of this role requires an understanding by attorneys of their relationship to our legal system. The Maryland Attorneys' Rules of Professional Conduct, when properly applied, serve to define that relationship.

Scope

[14] The Maryland Attorneys' Rules of Professional Conduct are rules of reason. They should be interpreted with reference to the purposes of legal representation and of the law itself. Some of the Rules are imperatives, cast in the terms "shall" or "shall not." These define proper conduct for purposes of professional discipline. Others, generally cast in the term "may," are permissive and define areas under the Rules in which the attorney has discretion to exercise professional judgment. No disciplinary action should be taken when the attorney chooses not to act or acts within the bounds of such discretion. Other Rules define the nature of relationships between the attorney and others. The Rules are thus partly obligatory and disciplinary and partly constitutive and descriptive in that they define a attorney's professional role. Many of the Comments use the term "should." Comments do not add obligations to the Rules but provide guidance for practicing in compliance with the Rules.

[15] The Rules presuppose a larger legal context shaping the attorney's role. That context includes court rules and statutes relating to matters of licensure, laws defining specific obligations of attorneys and substantive and procedural law in general. The Comments are sometimes used to alert attorneys to their responsibilities under such other law.

[16] Compliance with the Rules, as with all law in an open society, depends primarily upon understanding and voluntary compliance, secondarily upon reinforcement by peer and public opinion and finally, when necessary, upon enforcement through disciplinary proceedings. The Rules do not, however, exhaust the moral and ethical considerations that should inform an attorney, for no worthwhile human activity can be completely defined by legal rules. The Rules simply provide a framework for the ethical practice of law.

[17] Furthermore, for purposes of determining the attorney's authority and responsibility, principles of substantive law external to these Rules determine whether a client-attorney relationship exists. Most of the duties flowing from the client-attorney relationship attach only after the client has requested the attorney to render legal services and the attorney has agreed to do so. But there are some duties, such as that of confidentiality under Rule 19–301.6 (1.6), that attach when the attorney agrees to consider whether a client-attorney relationship shall be established. See Rule 19–301.18 (1.18). Whether a client-attorney relationship exists for any specific purpose can depend on the circumstances and may be a question of fact.

[18] Under various legal provisions, including constitutional, statutory and common law, the responsibilities of government attorneys may include authority concerning legal matters that ordinarily reposes in the client in private client-attorney relationships. For example, an attorney for a government agency may have authority on behalf of the government to decide upon settlement or whether to appeal from an adverse judgment. Such authority in various respects is generally vested in the attorney general and the state's attorney in state government, and their federal counterparts, and the same may be true of other government law officers. Also, attorneys under the

supervision of these officers may be authorized to represent several government agencies in intra-governmental legal controversies in circumstances where a private attorney could not represent multiple private clients. These Rules do not abrogate any such authority.

[19] Failure to comply with an obligation or prohibition imposed by a Rule is a basis for invoking the disciplinary process. The Rules presuppose that disciplinary assessment of an attorney's conduct will be made on the basis of the facts and circumstances as they existed at the time of the conduct in question and in recognition of the fact that an attorney often has to act upon uncertain or incomplete evidence of the situation. Moreover, the Rules presuppose that whether or not discipline should be imposed for a violation, and the severity of a sanction, depend on all the circumstances, such as the willfulness and seriousness of the violation, extenuating factors and whether there have been previous violations.

[20] Violation of a Rule does not itself give rise to a cause of action against an attorney nor does it create any presumption that a legal duty has been breached. In addition, violation of a Rule does not necessarily warrant any other non-disciplinary remedy, such as disqualification of an attorney in pending litigation. The Rules are designed to provide guidance to attorneys and to provide a structure for regulating conduct through disciplinary agencies. They are not designed to be a basis for civil liability. Furthermore, the purpose of the Rules can be subverted when they are invoked by opposing parties as procedural weapons. The fact that a Rule is a just basis for an attorney's self-assessment, or for sanctioning an attorney under the administration of a disciplinary authority, does not imply that an antagonist in a collateral proceeding or transaction has standing to seek enforcement of the Rule. Nevertheless, in some circumstances, an attorney's violation of a Rule may the applicable standard of conduct. Nothing in this Preamble and Scope is intended to detract from the holdings of the Supreme Court in *Post v. Bregman*, 349 Md. 142 (1998) and *Son v. Margolius, Mallios, Davis, Rider & Tomar*, 349 Md. 441 (1998).

[21] The Comment accompanying each Rule explains and illustrates the meaning and purpose of the Rule. The Preamble and this note on Scope provide general orientation. The Comments are intended as guides to interpretation, but the text of each Rule is authoritative.

[22] Rather than continue the practice of having all of the Maryland Attorneys' Rules of Professional Conduct (MARPC) incorporated into one Maryland Rule, each Rule is made a separate Maryland Rule, as each relates to a different topic. They all follow the numbering format of the American Bar Association Model Rules, however, and, for consistency, may be cited in that format, with the Maryland Rule designation in parenthesis. As an example, Rule 19–301.3 may be cited as MARPC 1.3 (Md. Rule 19–301.3).

RULE 1.0

TERMINOLOGY

(a) "Belief" or "believes" denotes that the person involved actually supposed the fact in question to be true. A person's belief may be inferred from circumstances.

(b) "Confirmed in writing," when used in reference to the informed consent of a person, denotes informed consent that is given in writing by the person or a writing that an attorney promptly transmits to the person confirming an oral informed consent. See section (g) of this Rule for the definition of "informed consent." If it is not feasible to obtain or transmit the writing at the time the person gives informed consent, then the attorney must obtain or transmit it within a reasonable time thereafter.

(c) "Consult" or "consultation" denotes communication of information reasonably sufficient to permit the client to appreciate the significance of the matter in question.

(d) "Diminished capacity" means a decreased ability to receive and understand information, evaluate that information, or make or communicate decisions, even with appropriate supports or accommodations, whether because of minority, mental impairment, or some other reason.

(e) "Firm" or "law firm" denotes:

(1) an association of an attorney or attorneys in a law partnership, professional corporation, sole proprietorship or other association formed for the practice of law; or

(2) a legal services organization or the legal department of a corporation, government, or other organization.

(f) "Fraud" or "fraudulent" denotes conduct that is fraudulent under the substantive or procedural law of the applicable jurisdiction and has a purpose to deceive.

(g) "Informed consent" denotes the agreement by a person to a proposed course of conduct after the attorney has communicated adequate information and explanation about the material risks of and reasonably available alternatives to the proposed course of conduct.

(h) "Knowingly," "known," or "knows" denotes actual knowledge of the fact in question. A person's knowledge may be inferred from circumstances.

(i) "Law firm" has the meaning stated in section (e) of this Rule.

(j) "Partner" denotes a member of a partnership, a shareholder in a law firm organized as a professional corporation, or a member of an association authorized to practice law.

(k) "Reasonable" or "reasonably" when used in relation to conduct by an attorney denotes the conduct of a reasonably prudent and competent attorney.

(l) "Reasonable belief" or "reasonably believes" when used in reference to an attorney denotes that the attorney believes the matter in question and that the circumstances are such that the belief is reasonable.

(m) "Reasonably should know" when used in reference to an attorney denotes that an attorney of reasonable prudence and competence would ascertain the matter in question.

(n) "Screened" denotes the isolation of an attorney from any participation in a matter through the timely imposition of procedures within a firm that are reasonably adequate under the circumstances to protect information that the isolated attorney is obligated to protect under these Rules or other law.

(o) "Substantial" when used in reference to degree or extent denotes a material matter of clear and weighty importance.

(p) "Tribunal" denotes a court, an arbitrator in a binding arbitration proceeding or a legislative body, administrative agency, or other body acting in an adjudicative capacity. A legislative body, administrative agency, or other body acts in an adjudicative capacity when a neutral official, after the presentation of evidence or legal argument by a party or parties, will render a binding legal decision directly affecting a party's interests in a particular matter.

(q) "Writing" or "written" denotes a tangible or electronic record of a communication or representation, including handwriting, typewriting, printing, photostating, photography, audio or video-recording, and e-mail. A "signed" writing includes an electronic sound, symbol, or process attached to or logically associated with a writing and executed or adopted by a person with the intent to sign the writing.

COMMENT

Confirmed in Writing

[1] If it is not feasible to obtain or transmit a written confirmation at the time the client gives informed consent, then the attorney must obtain or transmit it within a reasonable time thereafter. If an attorney has obtained a client's informed consent, the attorney may act in reliance on that consent so long as it is confirmed in writing within a reasonable time thereafter.

Diminished Capacity

[2] When an attorney is presented with signs that a client is or appears to be struggling with the ability to receive, understand, or process information, a "decreased ability" may be present. Examples of factors that could impede an individual's decision-making include a minor's age, a temporary or permanent mental impairment, addiction, and physical or emotional trauma. In some cases, a decreased ability may be alleviated or eliminated by the use of supports and accommodations that maximize the ability to make, communicate, or effectuate the client's own decisions. Examples of supports

and accommodations include effective communication devices or services, using assistance of appropriate third parties, providing an environment supportive of the client's abilities, and modifying the attorney's communication and counseling technique with the client. See generally Americans with Disabilities Act, 42 U.S.C. §§ 12101, et seq. Diminished capacity can be situational in nature, varying in degree, or affect some but not all decision. See Rule 19–301.14 (1.14).

Firm

[3] Whether two or more attorneys constitute a firm within section (e) of this Rule can depend on the specific facts. For example, two practitioners who share office space and occasionally consult or assist each other ordinarily would not be regarded as constituting a firm. However, if they present themselves to the public in a way that suggests that they are a firm or conduct themselves as a firm, they should be regarded as a firm for purposes of the Rules. The terms of any formal agreement between associated attorneys are relevant in determining whether they are a firm, as is the fact that they have mutual access to information concerning the clients they serve. Furthermore, it is relevant in doubtful cases to consider the underlying purpose of the Rule that is involved. A group of attorneys could be regarded as a firm for purposes of the Rule providing that the same attorney should not represent opposing parties in litigation, while it might not be so regarded for purposes of the Rule that information acquired by one attorney is attributed to another.

[4] With respect to the law department of an organization, including the government, there is ordinarily no question that the members of the department constitute a firm within the meaning of the Maryland Attorneys' Rules of Professional Conduct. There can be uncertainty, however, as to the identity of the client. For example, it may not be clear whether the law department of a corporation represents a subsidiary or an affiliated corporation, as well as the corporation by which the members of the department are directly employed. A similar question can arise concerning an unincorporated association and its local affiliates.

[5] Similar questions can also arise with respect to attorneys in legal aid and legal services organizations. Depending upon the structure of the organization, the entire organization or different components of it may constitute a firm or firms for purposes of these Rules.

Fraud

[6] When used in these Rules, the terms "fraud" or "fraudulent" refer to conduct that is characterized as such under the substantive or procedural law of the applicable jurisdiction and has a purpose to deceive. This does not include merely negligent misrepresentation or negligent failure to apprise another of relevant information. For purposes of these Rules, it is not necessary that anyone has suffered damages or relied on the misrepresentation or failure to inform.

Informed Consent

[7] Many of the Maryland Attorneys' Rules of Professional Conduct require the attorney to obtain the informed consent of a client or other person (e.g., a former client or, under certain circumstances, a prospective client) before accepting or continuing representation or pursuing a course of conduct. See, e.g., Rules 19–301.2 (c) (1.2), 19–301.6 (a) (1.6) and 19–301.7 (b) (1.7). The communication necessary to obtain such consent will vary according to the Rule involved and the circumstances giving rise to the need to obtain informed consent. The attorney must make reasonable efforts to ensure that the client or other person possesses information reasonably adequate to make an informed decision. Ordinarily, this will require communication that includes a disclosure of the facts and circumstances giving rise to the situation, any explanation reasonably necessary to inform the client or other person of the material advantages and disadvantages of the proposed course of conduct and a discussion of the client's or other person's options and alternatives. In some circumstances it may be appropriate for an attorney to advise a client or other person of facts or implications already known to the client or other person to seek the advice of another attorney. An attorney need not inform a client or other person of facts or implications already

known to the client or other person; nevertheless, an attorney who does not personally inform the client or other person assumes the risk that the client or other person is inadequately informed and the consent is invalid. In determining whether the information and explanation provided are reasonably adequate, relevant factors include whether the client or other person is experienced in legal matters generally and in making decisions of the type involved, and whether the client or other person is independently represented by another attorney in giving the consent. Normally, such persons need less information and explanation than others, and generally a client or other person who is independently represented by another attorney in giving the consent should be assumed to have given informed consent.

[8] Obtaining informed consent will usually require an affirmative response by the client or other person. In general, an attorney may not assume consent from a client's or other person's silence. Consent may be inferred, however, from the conduct of the client or other person who has reasonably adequate information about the matter. A number of Rules require that a person's consent be confirmed in writing. See Rules 19–301.7 (b) (1.7) and 19–301.9 (a) (1.9). For a definition of "writing" and "confirmed in writing," see sections (q) and (b) of this Rule. Other Rules require that a client's consent be obtained in a writing signed by the client. See, e.g., Rules 19–301.5 (c) (1.5) and 19–301.8 (a) (1.8). For a definition of "signed," see section (q) of this Rule.

Screened

[9] This definition applies to situations where screening of a personally disqualified attorney is permitted to remove imputation of a conflict of interest under Rules 19–301.10 (1.10), 19–301.11 (1.11), 19–301.12 (1.12), or 19–301.18 (1.18).

[10] The purpose of screening is to assure the affected parties that confidential information known by the personally disqualified attorney remains protected. The personally disqualified attorney should acknowledge the obligation not to communicate with any

of the other attorneys in the firm with respect to the matter. Similarly, other attorneys in the firm who are working on the matter should be informed that the screening is in place and that they may not communicate with the personally disqualified attorney with respect to the matter. Additional screening measures that are appropriate for the particular matter will depend on the circumstances. To implement, reinforce, and remind all affected attorneys of the presence of the screening, it may be appropriate for the firm to undertake such procedures as a written undertaking by the screened attorney to avoid any communication with other firm personnel and any contact with any firm files or other materials relating to the matter, written notice and instructions to all other firm personnel forbidding any communication with the screened attorney relating to the matter, denial of access by the screened attorney to firm files or other materials relating to the matter, and periodic reminders of the screen to the screened attorney and all other firm personnel.

[11] In order to be effective, screening measures must be implemented as soon as practical after an attorney or law firm knows or reasonably should know that there is a need for screening.

♦ ♦ ♦

Model Rules Comparison—Rule 19–301.0 (1.0) is substantially similar to the language of the Ethics 2000 Amendments to the ABA Model Rules of Professional Conduct except for the retention of the definition of "consult" and "consultation," the addition of the definition of "diminished capacity," the addition of a cross reference to "law firm," and the appropriate redesignation of sections.

CLIENT-ATTORNEY RELATIONSHIP

RULE 1.1

COMPETENCE

An attorney shall provide competent representation to a client. Competent representation requires the legal knowledge, skill, thoroughness and preparation reasonably necessary for the representation.

COMMENT

Legal knowledge and skill

[1] In determining whether an attorney employs the requisite knowledge and skill in a particular matter, relevant factors include the relative complexity and specialized nature of the matter, the attorney's general experience, the attorney's training and experience in the field in question, the preparation and study the attorney is able to give the matter and whether it is feasible to refer the matter to, or associate or consult with, an attorney of established competence in the field in question. In many instances, the required proficiency is that of a general practitioner. Expertise in a particular field of law may be required in some circumstances.

[2] An attorney need not necessarily have special training or prior experience to handle legal problems of a type with which the attorney is unfamiliar. A newly admitted attorney can be as competent as a practitioner with long experience. Some important legal skills, such as the analysis of precedent, the evaluation of evidence and legal drafting, are required in all legal problems. Perhaps the most fundamental legal skill consists of determining what kind of legal problems a situation may involve, a skill that necessarily transcends any particular specialized knowledge. An attorney can provide adequate representation in a wholly novel field through necessary study. Competent representation can also be provided through the association of an attorney of established competence in the field in question.

[3] In an emergency an attorney may give advice or assistance in a matter in which the attorney does not have the skill ordinarily required where referral to or consultation or association with another attorney would be impractical. Even in an emergency, however, assistance should be limited to that reasonably necessary in the circumstances, for ill-considered action under emergency conditions can jeopardize the client's interest.

[4] An attorney may accept representation where the requisite level of competence can be achieved by reasonable preparation. This applies as well to an attorney who is appointed as an attorney for an unrepresented person. See also Rule 19–306.2 (6.2).

Thoroughness and preparation

[5] Competent handling of a particular matter includes inquiry into and analysis of the factual and legal elements of the problem, and use of methods and procedures meeting the standards of competent practitioners. It also includes adequate preparation. The required attention and preparation are determined in part by what is at stake; major litigation and complex transactions ordinarily require more extensive treatment than matters of lesser complexity. An agreement between the attorney and the client regarding the scope of the representation may limit the matters for which the attorney is responsible. See Rule 19–301.2 (c) (1.2).

Maintaining competence

[6] To maintain the requisite knowledge and skill, an attorney should keep abreast of changes in the law and its practice, engage in continuing study and education and comply with all continuing legal education requirements to which the attorney is subject.

♦ ♦ ♦

Model Rules Comparison: Rule 19–301.1 (1.1) is substantially similar to the language of the Ethics 2000 Amendments to the ABA Model Rules of Professional Conduct.

RULE 1.2

Scope of Representation and Allocation of Authority Between Client and Attorney

(a) Subject to sections (c) and (d) of this Rule, an attorney shall abide by a client's decisions concerning the objectives of the representation and, when appropriate, shall consult with the client as to the means by which they are to be pursued. An attorney may take such action on behalf of the client as is impliedly authorized to carry out the representation. An attorney shall abide by a client's decision whether to settle a matter. In a criminal case, the attorney shall abide by the client's decision, after consultation with the attorney, as to a plea to be entered, whether to waive jury trial and whether the client will testify.

(b) An attorney's representation of a client, including representation by appointment, does not constitute an endorsement of the client's political, economic, social or moral views or activities.

(c) An attorney may limit the scope of the representation in accordance with applicable Maryland Rules if (1) the limitation is reasonable under the circumstances, (2) the client gives informed consent, and (3) the scope and limitations of any representation, beyond an initial consultation or brief advice provided without a fee, are clearly set forth in a writing, including any duty on the part of the attorney under Rule 1–324 to forward notices to the client.

(d) An attorney shall not counsel a client to engage, or assist a client, in conduct that the attorney knows is criminal or fraudulent, but an attorney may discuss the legal consequences of any proposed course of conduct with a client and may counsel or assist a client to make a good faith effort to determine the validity, scope, meaning or application of the law.

COMMENT

Scope of Representation

[1] Both attorney and client have authority and responsibility in the objectives and means of representation. The client has ultimate authority to determine the purposes to be served by legal representation, within the limits imposed by law and the attorney's professional obligations. Within those limits, a client also has a right to consult with the attorney about the means to be used in pursuing those objectives. At the same time, an attorney is not required to pursue objectives or employ means simply because a client may wish that the attorney do so. A clear distinction between objectives and means sometimes cannot be drawn, and in many cases the client-attorney relationship partakes of a joint undertaking. In questions of means, the attorney should assume responsibility for technical and legal tactical issues, but should defer to the client regarding such questions as the expense to be incurred and concern for third persons who might be adversely affected.

[2] On occasion, however, an attorney and a client may disagree about the means to be used to accomplish the client's objectives. Because of the varied nature of the matters about which an attorney and client might disagree and because the actions in question may implicate the interests of a tribunal or other persons, this Rule does not prescribe how such disagreements are to be resolved. Other law, however, may be applicable and should be consulted by the attorney. The attorney should also consult with the client and seek a mutually acceptable resolution of the disagreement. If such efforts are unavailing and the attorney has a fundamental disagreement with the client, the attorney may withdraw from the representation. See Rule 19–301.16 (b)(4) (1.16). Conversely, the client may resolve the disagreement by discharging the attorney. See Rule 19–301.16 (a)(3) (1.16).

[3] At the outset of a representation, the client may authorize the attorney to take specific action on the client's behalf without further consultation. Absent a material change in circumstances and subject to Rule 19–301.4 (1.4), an attorney may rely on such an advance authorization. The client may, however, revoke such authority at any time.

[4] In a case in which the client appears to be suffering diminished capacity, the attorney's duty to abide by the client's decisions is to be guided by reference to Rule 19–301.14 (1.14).

Independence from Client's Views or Activities

[5] Legal representation should not be denied to people who are unable to afford legal services, or whose cause is controversial or the subject of popular disapproval. By the same token, representing a client does not constitute approval of the client's views or activities.

Agreements Limiting Scope of Representation

[6] The scope of services to be provided by an attorney may be limited by agreement with the client or by the terms under which the attorney's services are made available to the client. When an attorney has been retained by an insurer to represent an insured, for

example, the representation may be limited to matters related to the insurance coverage. A limited representation may be appropriate because the client has limited objectives for the representation. In addition, the terms upon which representation is undertaken may exclude specific means that might otherwise be used to accomplish the client's objectives. Such limitations may exclude actions that the client thinks are too costly or that the attorney regards as repugnant or imprudent.

[7] Although this Rule affords the attorney and client substantial latitude to limit the representation, the limitation must be reasonable under the circumstances. If, for example, a client's objective is limited to securing general information about the law the client needs in order to handle a common and typically uncomplicated legal problem, the attorney and client may agree that the attorney's services will be limited to a brief telephone consultation. Such a limitation, however, would not be reasonable if the time allotted was not sufficient to yield advice upon which the client could rely. Although an agreement for a limited representation does not exempt an attorney from the duty to provide competent representation, the limitation is a factor to be considered when determining the legal knowledge, skill, thoroughness and preparation reasonably necessary for the representation. See Rule 19–301.1 (1.1).

[8] An attorney and a client may agree that the scope of the representation is to be limited to clearly defined specific tasks or objectives, including: (1) without entering an appearance, filing papers, or otherwise participating on the client's behalf in any judicial or administrative proceeding, (i) giving legal advice to the client regarding the client's rights, responsibilities, or obligations with respect to particular matters, (ii) conducting factual investigations for the client, (iii) representing the client in settlement negotiations or in private alternative dispute resolution proceedings, (iv) evaluating and advising the client with regard to settlement options or proposed agreements, or (v) drafting documents, performing legal research, and providing advice that the client or another attorney appearing for the client may use in a judicial or administrative proceeding; or (2) in accordance with applicable Maryland Rules, representing the

client in discrete judicial or administrative proceedings, such as a court- ordered alternative dispute resolution proceeding, a pendente lite proceeding, or proceedings on a temporary restraining order, a particular motion, or a specific issue in a multi-issue action or proceeding. Before entering into such an agreement, the attorney shall fully and fairly inform the client of the extent and limits of the attorney's obligations under the agreement, including any duty on the part of the attorney under Rule 1–324 to forward notices to the client.

[9] Representation of a client in a collaborative law process is a type of permissible limited representation. It requires a collaborative law participation agreement that complies with the requirements of Code, Courts Article, § 3–1902 and Rule 17–503 (b) and is signed by all parties after informed consent.

[10] All agreements concerning an attorney's representation of a client must accord with the Maryland Attorneys' Rules of Professional Conduct and other law. See, e.g., Rule 19–301.1 (1.1), 19–301.8 (1.8) and 19–305.6 (5.6).

Criminal, Fraudulent and Prohibited Transactions

[11] Section (d) of this Rule prohibits an attorney from knowingly counseling or assisting a client to commit a crime or fraud. This prohibition, however, does not preclude the attorney from giving an honest opinion about the actual consequences that appear likely to result from a client's conduct. The fact that a client uses advice in a course of action that is criminal or fraudulent does not, of itself, make an attorney a party to the course of action. There is a critical distinction between presenting an analysis of legal aspects of questionable conduct and recommending the means by which a crime or fraud might be committed with impunity.

[12] Maryland enacted a medical marijuana law in 2013. See Code, Health General Article, § 13–3301 et seq. As a matter of State law, some medical marijuana activities are permissible, and are subject to regulation. Notwithstanding Maryland law, the Federal Controlled Substances Act, 21 U.S.C. §§ 801–904, continues to criminalize the production, use, and distribution of marijuana, even in the context

of medical use. As of 2014, the federal government has taken the position, however, that it generally does not wish to interfere with retail sales of medical marijuana permitted under State law.

♦ ♦ ♦

In this narrow context, an attorney may counsel a client about compliance with the State's medical marijuana law without violating Rule 19–301.2 (d) and provide legal services in connection with business activities permitted by the State statute, provided that the attorney also advises the client about the legal consequences, under other applicable law, of the client's proposed course of conduct.

♦ ♦ ♦

[13] When the client's course of action has already begun and is continuing, the attorney's responsibility is especially delicate. The attorney is required to avoid assisting the client, for example, by drafting or delivering documents that the attorney knows are fraudulent or by suggesting how the wrongdoing might be concealed. An attorney may not continue assisting a client in conduct that the attorney originally supposed was legally proper but then discovers is criminal or fraudulent. The attorney must, therefore, withdraw from the representation of the client in the matter. See Rule 19–301.16 (a) (1.16). In some cases withdrawal alone might be insufficient. It may be necessary for the attorney to give notice of the fact of withdrawal and to disaffirm any opinion, document, affirmation or the like. See Rules 19–301.6 (1.6), 19–304.1 (4.1).

[14] Where the client is a fiduciary, the attorney may be charged with special obligations in dealings with a beneficiary.

[15] Section (d) of this Rule applies whether or not the defrauded party is a party to the transaction. Hence, an attorney must not participate in a transaction to effectuate criminal or fraudulent avoidance of tax liability. Section (d) does not preclude undertaking a criminal defense incident to a general retainer for legal services to a lawful enterprise. The last clause of section (d) of this Rule recognizes that determining the validity or interpretation of a statute or regulation may require a course of action involving disobedience of the statute or regulation or of the interpretation placed upon it by governmental authorities.

[16] If an attorney comes to know or reasonably should know that a client expects assistance not permitted by the Maryland Attorneys' Rules of Professional Conduct or other law or if the attorney intends to act contrary to the client's instructions, the attorney must consult with the client regarding the limitations on the attorney's conduct. See Rule 19–301.4 (a)(4) (1.4).

♦ ♦ ♦

Model Rules Comparison—Rule 19–301.2 (1.2) is substantially similar to the language of the Ethics 2000 Amendments to the ABA Model Rules of Professional Conduct except for wording changes in Rule 19–301.2 (a) (1.2), the addition of Comments [8], [9], and [12], and the retention of existing Maryland language in Comment [1].

RULE 1.3

DILIGENCE

An attorney shall act with reasonable diligence and promptness in representing a client.

COMMENT

[1] An attorney should pursue a matter on behalf of a client despite opposition, obstruction or personal inconvenience to the attorney, and may take whatever lawful and ethical measures are required to vindicate a client's cause or endeavor. An attorney must also act with commitment and dedication to the interests of the client and with zeal in advocacy upon the client's behalf. An attorney is not bound, however, to press for every advantage that might be realized for a client. For example, an attorney may have authority to exercise professional discretion in determining the means by which a matter should be pursued. See Rule 19–301.2 (1.2). The attorney's duty to act with reasonable diligence does not require the use of offensive tactics or permit treating any person involved in the legal process without courtesy and respect.

[2] An attorney's workload must be controlled so that each matter can be handled competently.

[3] Perhaps no professional shortcoming is more widely resented than procrastination. A client's interests often can be adversely affected by the passage of time or the change of conditions; in extreme instances, as when an attorney overlooks a statute of limitations, the client's legal position may be destroyed. Even when the client's interests are not affected in substance, however, unreasonable delay can cause a client needless anxiety and undermine confidence in the attorney's trustworthiness. An attorney's duty to act with reasonable promptness, however, does not preclude the attorney from agreeing to a reasonable request for a postponement that will not prejudice the attorney's client.

[4] Unless the relationship is terminated as provided in Rule 19–301.16 (1.16), an attorney should carry through to conclusion all matters undertaken for a client. If an attorney's employment is limited to a specific matter, the relationship terminates when the matter has been resolved. If an attorney has served a client over a substantial period in a variety of matters, the client sometimes may assume that the attorney will continue to serve on a continuing basis unless the attorney gives notice of withdrawal. Doubt about whether a client-attorney relationship still exists should be clarified by the attorney, preferably in writing, so that the client will not mistakenly suppose the attorney is looking after the client's affairs when the attorney has ceased to do so. For example, if an attorney has handled a judicial or administrative proceeding that produced a result adverse to the client and the attorney and client have not agreed that the attorney will handle the matter on appeal, the attorney must consult with the client about the possibility of appeal before relinquishing responsibility for the matter. See Rule 19–301.4 (1.4). Similarly, the attorney must inform the client if, following a result favorable to the client, another party files an appeal. Whether the attorney is obligated to prosecute the appeal for the client depends on the scope of the representation the attorney has agreed to provide to the client. See Rule 19–301.2 (1.2).

[5] To prevent neglect of client matters in the event of a sole practitioner's death or disability, the duty of diligence may require that each sole practitioner prepare a plan, in conformity with applicable rules, that

designates another competent attorney to review client files, notify each client of the attorney's death or disability, and determine whether there is a need for immediate protective action. Cf. Md. Rule 19–734 (providing for appointment of a conservator to inventory the files of an attorney who is deceased or has abandoned the practice of law, and to take other appropriate action to protect the attorney's clients in the absence of a plan to protect clients' interests).

♦ ♦ ♦

Model Rules Comparison: Rule 19–301.3 (1.3) is substantially similar to the language of the Ethics 2000 Amendments to the ABA Model Rules of Professional Conduct except for Comment [5], which incorporates Maryland law.

RULE 1.4

COMMUNICATION

(a) An attorney shall:

(1) promptly inform the client of any decision or circumstance with respect to which the client's informed consent, as defined in Rule 19–301.0(g) (1.0), is required by these Rules;

(2) keep the client reasonably informed about the status of the matter;

(3) promptly comply with reasonable requests for information; and

(4) consult with the client about any relevant limitation on the attorney's conduct when the attorney knows that the client expects assistance not permitted by the Maryland Attorneys' Rules of Professional Conduct or other law.

(b) An attorney shall explain a matter to the extent reasonably necessary to permit the client to make informed decisions regarding the representation.

COMMENT

[1] Reasonable communication between the attorney and the client is necessary for the client effectively to participate in the representation.

Communicating with Client

[2] If these Rules require that a particular decision about the representation be made by the client, subsection (a)(1) of this Rule requires that the attorney promptly consult with and secure the client's consent prior to taking action unless prior discussions with the client have resolved what action the client wants the attorney to take. For example, an attorney who receives from an opposing attorney an offer of settlement in a civil controversy or a proffered plea bargain in a criminal case must promptly inform the client of its substance unless the client has previously indicated that the proposal will be acceptable or unacceptable or has authorized the attorney to accept or to reject the offer. See Rule 19–301.2 (a) (1.2).

[3] Under Rule 19–301.2 (a) (1.2), an attorney is required, when appropriate, to consult with the client about the means to be used to accomplish the client's objectives. In some situations—depending on both the importance of the action under consideration and the feasibility of consulting with the client—this duty will require consultation prior to taking action. In other circumstances, such as during a trial when an immediate decision must be made, the exigency of the situation may require the attorney to act without prior consultation. In such cases the attorney must nonetheless act reasonably to inform the client of actions the attorney has taken on the client's behalf. Additionally, subsection (a)(2) of this Rule requires that the attorney keep the client reasonably informed about the status of the matter, such as significant developments affecting the timing or the substance of the representation.

[4] An attorney's regular communication with clients will minimize the occasions on which a client will need to request information concerning the representation. When a client makes a reasonable request for information, however, subsection (a)(3) of this Rule requires prompt compliance with the request, or if a prompt response is not feasible, that the attorney, or a member of the attorney's staff, acknowledge receipt of the request and advise the client when a response may be expected. Client telephone calls should be promptly returned or acknowledged.

Explaining Matters

[5] The client should have sufficient information to participate intelligently in decisions concerning the objectives of the representation and the means by which they are to be pursued, to the extent the client is willing and able to do so. Adequacy of communication depends in part on the kind of advice or assistance that is involved. For example, where there is time to explain a proposal made in a negotiation, the attorney should review all important provisions with the client before proceeding to an agreement. In litigation an attorney should explain the general strategy and prospects of success and ordinarily should consult the client on tactics that are likely to result in significant expense or to injure or coerce others. On the other hand, an attorney ordinarily will not be expected to describe trial or negotiation strategy in detail. The guiding principle is that the attorney should fulfill reasonable client expectations for information consistent with the duty to act in the client's best interests, and the client's overall requirements as to the character of representation. In certain circumstances, such as when an attorney asks a client to consent to a representation affected by a conflict of interest, the client must give informed consent, as defined in Rule 19–301.0(g) (1.0).

[6] Ordinarily, the information to be provided is that appropriate for a client who is a comprehending and responsible adult. However, fully informing the client according to this standard may be impracticable, for example, where the client is a child or has diminished capacity. See Rule 19–301.14 (1.14). When a third party is used to facilitate communication as part of the representation, the attorney should guard against the possibility of bias or undue influence on the part of the facilitator. When the client is an organization or group, it is often impossible or inappropriate to inform every one of its members about its legal affairs; ordinarily, the attorney should address communications to the appropriate officials of the organization. See Rule 19–301.13 (1.13). Where many routine matters are involved, a system of limited or occasional reporting may be arranged with the client.

Withholding Information

[7] In some circumstances, an attorney may be justified in delaying transmission of information when the client would be likely to react imprudently to an immediate communication. Thus, an attorney might withhold a psychiatric diagnosis of a client when the examining psychiatrist indicates that disclosure would harm the client. An attorney may not withhold information to serve the attorney's own interest or convenience or the interests or convenience of another person. Rules or court orders governing litigation may provide that information supplied to an attorney may not be disclosed to the client. Rule 19–303.4 (c) (3.4) directs compliance with such rules or orders.

♦ ♦ ♦

Model Rules Comparison: Rule 19–301.4 (1.4) is substantially similar to the language of the Ethics 2000 Amendments to the ABA Model Rules of Professional Conduct except for the deletion of Model Rule 1.4 (a)(2) and the redesignation of subsections as appropriate, wording changes to Comment [3], and additions to Comment [6].

RULE 1.5

FEES

(a) An attorney shall not make an agreement for, charge, or collect an unreasonable fee or an unreasonable amount for expenses. The factors to be considered in determining the reasonableness of a fee include the following:

(1) the time and labor required, the novelty and difficulty of the questions involved, and the skill requisite to perform the legal service properly;

(2) the likelihood, if apparent to the client, that the acceptance of the particular employment will preclude other employment of the attorney;

(3) the fee customarily charged in the locality for similar legal services;

(4) the amount involved and the results obtained;

(5) the time limitations imposed by the client or by the circumstances;

(6) the nature and length of the professional relationship with the client;

(7) the experience, reputation, and ability of the attorney or attorneys performing the services; and

(8) whether the fee is fixed or contingent.

(b) The scope of the representation and the basis or rate of the fee and expenses for which the client will be responsible shall be communicated to the client, preferably in writing, before or within a reasonable time after commencing the representation, except when the attorney will charge a regularly represented client on the same basis or rate. Any changes in the basis or rate of the fee or expenses shall also be communicated to the client.

(c) A fee may be contingent on the outcome of the matter for which the service is rendered, except in a matter in which a contingent fee is prohibited by section (d) of this Rule or other law. A contingent fee agreement shall be in a writing signed by the client and shall state the method by which the fee is to be determined, including the percentage or percentages that shall accrue to the attorney in the event of settlement, trial or appeal; litigation and other expenses to be deducted from the recovery; and whether such expenses are to be deducted before or after the contingent fee is calculated. The agreement must clearly notify the client of any expenses for which the client will be responsible whether or not the client is the prevailing party. Upon conclusion of a contingent fee matter, the attorney shall provide the client with a written statement stating the outcome of the matter, and, if there is a recovery, showing the remittance to the client and the method of its determination.

(d) An attorney shall not enter into an arrangement for, charge, or collect:

(1) any fee in a domestic relations matter, the payment or amount of which is contingent upon the securing of a divorce or custody of a child or upon the amount of alimony or support or property settlement, or upon the amount of an award pursuant to Md. Code, Family Law Article, §§ 8–201 through 8–213; or

(2) a contingent fee for representing a defendant in a criminal case.

(e) A division of a fee between attorneys who are not in the same firm may be made only if:
  (1) the division is in proportion to the services performed by each attorney or each attorney assumes joint responsibility for the representation;
  (2) the client agrees to the joint representation and the agreement is confirmed in writing; and
  (3) the total fee is reasonable.

COMMENT

Reasonableness of Fee and Expenses

[1] Section (a) of this Rule requires that attorneys charge fees that are reasonable under the circumstances. The factors specified in subsection (a)(1) through (8) of this Rule are not exclusive. Nor will each factor be relevant in each instance. Section (a) of this Rule also requires that expenses for which the client will be charged must be reasonable. An attorney may seek reimbursement for the cost of services performed in-house, such as copying, or for other expenses incurred in-house, such as telephone charges, either by charging a reasonable amount to which the client has agreed in advance or by charging an amount that reasonably reflects the cost incurred by the attorney.

Basis or Rate of Fee

[2] When the attorney has regularly represented a client, they ordinarily will have evolved an understanding concerning the basis or rate of the fee and the expenses for which the client will be responsible. In a new client-attorney relationship, however, an understanding as to fees and expenses must be promptly established. Generally, it is desirable to furnish the client with at least a simple memorandum or copy of the attorney's customary fee arrangements that states the general nature of the legal services to be provided, the basis, rate, or total amount of the fee and whether and to what extent the client will be responsible for any costs, expenses or disbursements in the course of representation.

A written statement concerning the terms of the engagement reduces the possibility of misunderstanding.

[3] Contingent fees, like any other fees, are subject to the reasonableness standard of section (a) of this Rule. In determining whether a particular contingent fee is reasonable, or whether it is reasonable to charge any form of contingent fee, an attorney must consider the factors that are relevant under the circumstances. Applicable law may impose limitations on contingent fees, such as a ceiling on the percentage allowable, or may require an attorney to offer clients an alternative basis for the fee. Applicable law may also apply to situations other than a contingent fee, for example, government regulations regarding fees in certain tax matters.

Terms of Payment

[4] An attorney may require advance payment of a fee, but is obliged to return any unearned portion. See Rule 19–301.15 (c) (1.15); Comment [3] to Rule 19–301.15 (1.15); Rule 19–301.16 (d) (1.16). An attorney may accept property in payment for services, such as an ownership interest in an enterprise, providing this does not involve acquisition of a proprietary interest in the cause of action or subject matter of the litigation contrary to Rule 19–301.8 (i) (1.8). However, a fee paid in property instead of money may be subject to the requirements of Rule 19–301.8 (a) (1.8) because such fees often have the essential qualities of a business transaction with the client.

[5] An agreement may not be made whose terms might induce the attorney improperly to curtail services for the client or perform them in a way contrary to the client's interest. For example, an attorney should not enter into an agreement whereby services are to be provided only up to a stated amount when it is foreseeable that more extensive services probably will be required, unless the situation is adequately explained to the client. Otherwise, the client might have to bargain for further assistance in the midst of a proceeding or transaction. However, it is proper to define the extent of services in light of the client's ability to pay. An attorney should not exploit a fee arrangement based primarily on hourly charges by using wasteful procedures.

Prohibited Contingent Fees

[6] Section (d) of this Rule prohibits an attorney from charging a contingent fee in a domestic relations matter when payment is contingent upon the securing of a divorce or upon the amount of alimony or support or property settlement to be obtained. This provision does not preclude a contract for a contingent fee for legal representation in connection with the recovery of post-judgment balances due under support, alimony or other financial orders because such contracts do not implicate the same policy concerns.

Division of Fee

[7] A division of fee is a single billing to a client covering the fee of two or more attorneys who are not in the same firm. A division of fee facilitates association of more than one attorney in a matter in which neither alone could serve the client as well, and most often is used when the fee is contingent and the division is between a referring attorney and a trial specialist. Section (e) of this Rule permits the attorneys to divide a fee on either the basis of the proportion of services they render or by agreement between the participating attorneys if all assume responsibility for the representation as a whole and the client agrees to the joint representation, which is confirmed in writing. Contingent fee agreements must be in a writing signed by the client and must otherwise comply with section (c) of this Rule. Joint responsibility for the representation entails financial and ethical responsibility for the representation as if the attorneys were associated in a partnership. An attorney should only refer a matter to an attorney whom the referring attorney reasonably believes is competent to handle the matter. See Rule 19–301.1 (1.1).

[8] Section (e) of this Rule does not prohibit or regulate division of fees to be received in the future for work done when attorneys were previously associated in a law firm.

Disputes over Fees

[9] If a procedure has been established for resolution of fee disputes, such as an arbitration or mediation procedure established by the bar, the attorney must comply with the procedure when it is mandatory,

and even when it is voluntary, the attorney should conscientiously consider submitting to it. Law may prescribe a procedure for determining an attorney's fee, for example, in representation of an executor or administrator, a class or a person entitled to a reasonable fee as part of the measure of damages. The attorney entitled to such a fee and an attorney representing another party concerned with the fee should comply with the prescribed procedure.

♦ ♦ ♦

Cross reference: See *Post v. Bregman*, 349 Md. 142 (1998) and *Son v. Margolius*, 349 Md. 441 (1998).

Model Rules Comparison: Rule 19–301.5 (1.5) is substantially similar to the language of the Ethics 2000 Amendments to the ABA Model Rules of Professional Conduct except that it retains existing Maryland language in Rule 19–301.5 (d)(1) (1.5) and adds wording changes to Rule 19–301.5 (e)(2) (1.5) and Comment [7].

RULE 1.6

CONFIDENTIALITY OF INFORMATION

(a) An attorney shall not reveal information relating to representation of a client unless the client gives informed consent, the disclosure is impliedly authorized in order to carry out the representation, or the disclosure is permitted by section (b) of this Rule.

(b) An attorney may reveal information relating to the representation of a client to the extent the attorney reasonably believes necessary:

(1) to prevent reasonably certain death or substantial bodily harm;

(2) to prevent the client from committing a crime or fraud that is reasonably certain to result in substantial injury to the financial interests or property of another and in furtherance of which the client has used or is using the attorney's services;

(3) to prevent, mitigate, or rectify substantial injury to the financial interests or property of another that is reasonably certain to result or has resulted from the client's commission of a crime or fraud in furtherance of which the client has used the attorney's services; to secure legal advice about the attorney's compliance with these Rules, a court order or other law;

(4) to establish a claim or defense on behalf of the attorney in a controversy between the attorney and the client, to establish a defense to a criminal charge, civil claim, or disciplinary complaint against the attorney based upon conduct in which the client was involved or to respond to allegations in any proceeding concerning the attorney's representation of the client; or

(5) to comply with these Rules, a court order or other law.

COMMENT

[1] This Rule governs the disclosure by an attorney of information relating to the representation of a client during the attorney's representation of the client. See Rule 19–301.18 (1.18) for the attorney's duties with respect to information provided to the attorney by a prospective client, Rule 19–301.9 (c)(2) (1.9) for the attorney's duty not to reveal information relating to the attorney's prior representation of a former client and Rules 19–301.8 (b) (1.8) and 19–301.9 (c)(1) (1.9) for the attorney's duties with respect to the use of such information to the disadvantage of clients and former clients.

[2] A fundamental principle in the client-attorney relationship is that, in the absence of the client's informed consent, the attorney must not reveal information relating to the representation. See Rule 19–301.0 (g) (1.0) for the definition of informed consent. This contributes to the trust that is the hallmark of the client-attorney relationship. The client is thereby encouraged to seek legal assistance and to communicate fully and frankly with the attorney even as to embarrassing or legally damaging subject matter. The attorney needs this information to represent the client effectively and, if necessary, to advise the client to refrain from wrongful conduct. Almost without exception, clients come to attorneys in order to determine their rights and what is, in the complex of laws and regulations, deemed to be legal and correct. Based upon experience, attorneys know that almost all clients follow the advice given, and the law is upheld.

[3] The principle of client-attorney confidentiality is given effect by related bodies of law: the attorney-client privilege, the work

product doctrine and the rule of confidentiality established in professional ethics. The attorney-client privilege and work- product doctrine apply in judicial and other proceedings in which an attorney may be called as a witness or otherwise required to produce evidence concerning a client. The rule of client-attorney confidentiality applies in situations other than those where evidence is sought from the attorney through compulsion of law. The confidentiality rule, for example, applies not only to matters communicated in confidence by the client but also to all information relating to the representation, whatever its source. An attorney may not disclose such information except as authorized or required by the Maryland Attorneys' Rules of Professional Conduct or other law. See also Scope.

[4] Section (a) of this Rule prohibits an attorney from revealing information relating to the representation of a client. This prohibition also applies to disclosures by an attorney that do not in themselves reveal protected information but could reasonably lead to the discovery of such information by a third person. An attorney's use of a hypothetical to discuss issues relating to the representation is permissible so long as there is no reasonable likelihood that the listener will be able to ascertain the identity of the client or the situation involved.

Implied Authority to Disclose

[5] Except to the extent that the client's instructions or special circumstances limit that authority, an attorney is impliedly authorized to make disclosures about a client when appropriate in carrying out the representation. In some situations, for example, an attorney may be impliedly authorized to admit a fact that cannot properly be disputed, or to make a disclosure that facilitates a satisfactory conclusion to a matter. Attorneys in a firm may, in the course of the firm's practice, disclose to each other information relating to a client of the firm, unless the client has instructed that particular information be confined to specified attorneys.

Disclosure Adverse to Client

[6] Although the public interest is usually best served by a strict rule requiring attorneys to preserve the confidentiality of information relating to the representation of their clients, the confidentiality rule is subject to limited exceptions. Section (b) of this Rule, however, permits disclosure only to the extent the attorney reasonably believes the disclosure is necessary to accomplish one of the purposes specified. Where practicable, the attorney should first seek to persuade the client to take suitable action to obviate the need for disclosure. In any case, a disclosure adverse to the client's interest should be no greater than the attorney reasonably believes necessary to accomplish the purpose. If the disclosure will be made in connection with a judicial proceeding, the disclosure should be made in a manner that limits access to the information to the tribunal or other persons having a need to know it and appropriate protective orders or other arrangements should be sought by the attorney to the fullest extent practicable.

[7] Section (b) of this Rule permits, but does not require the disclosure of information relating to a client's representation to accomplish the purposes specified in subsections (b)(1) through (b)(6) of this Rule. In exercising the discretion conferred by this Rule, the attorney may consider such factors as the nature of the attorney's relationship with the client and with those who might be injured by the client, the attorney's own involvement in the transaction and factors that may extenuate the conduct in question. An attorney's decision not to disclose as permitted by section (b) of this Rule does not violate this Rule. Disclosure may be required, however, by other Rules regardless of whether the disclosure is permitted by Rule 19–301.6 (1.6). See Rules 19–301.2 (d) (1.2), 19–303.3 (a)(4) (3.3), 19–304.1 (b) (4.1), 19–308.1 (8.1) and 19–308.3 (8.3). An attorney representing an organization may in some circumstances be permitted to disclose information regardless of whether the disclosure is permitted by Rule 19–301.6 (b) (1.6). See Rule 19–301.13 (c) (1.13).

[8] Subsection (b)(1) of this Rule recognizes the overriding value of life and physical integrity and permits disclosure reasonably believed necessary to prevent reasonably certain death or substantial bodily

harm. Such harm is reasonably certain to occur if it will be suffered imminently or if there is a present and substantial threat that a person will suffer such harm at a later date if the attorney fails to take action necessary to eliminate the threat. Thus, an attorney who knows that a client has accidentally discharged toxic waste into a town's water supply may reveal this information to the authorities if there is a present and substantial risk that a person who drinks the water will contract a life-threatening or debilitating disease, and the attorney reasonably believes disclosure is necessary to eliminate the threat or reduce the number of victims.

[9] Subsection (b)(2) of this Rule is a limited exception to the rule of confidentiality that permits the attorney to reveal information to the extent necessary to enable affected persons or appropriate authorities to prevent the client from committing a crime or a fraud, as defined in Rule 19–301.0 (f) (1.0), that is reasonably certain to result in substantial injury to the financial or property interests of another and in furtherance of which the client has used or is using the attorney's services. Such a serious abuse of the client-attorney relationship by the client forfeits the protection of this Rule. The client can, of course, prevent such disclosure by refraining from the wrongful conduct. Although subsection (b)(2) of this Rule does not require the attorney to reveal the client's misconduct, the attorney may not counsel or assist the client in conduct the attorney knows is criminal or fraudulent. See Rule 19–301.2 (d) (1.2). See also Rule 19–301.16 (1.16) with respect to the attorney's obligation or right to withdraw from the representation of the client in such circumstances. Where the client is an organization, the attorney should consult Rule 19–301.13 (b) (1.13).

[10] Subsection (b)(3) of this Rule addresses the situation in which the attorney does not learn of a client's criminal or fraudulent act in furtherance of which the attorney's services were used until after the act has occurred. Although the client no longer has the option of preventing disclosure by refraining from the wrongful conduct, there will be situations in which the loss suffered by the affected person can be prevented, rectified or mitigated. In such situations, the attorney may disclose information relating to the representation

to the extent necessary to enable the affected persons to prevent or mitigate reasonably certain losses or to attempt to recoup their losses. Subsection (b)(3) of this Rule does not apply when a person who has committed a crime or fraud thereafter employs an attorney for representation concerning that offense.

[11] An attorney's confidentiality obligations do not preclude an attorney from securing confidential legal advice about the attorney's personal responsibility to comply with these Rules, a court order or other law. In most situations, disclosing information to secure such advice will be impliedly authorized for the attorney to carry out the representation. Even when the disclosure is not impliedly authorized, subsection (b)(4) of this Rule permits such disclosure because of the importance of an attorney's compliance with the law.

Withdrawal

[12] If the attorney knows that the attorney's services will be used by the client in materially furthering a course of criminal or fraudulent conduct, the attorney must withdraw, as stated in Rule 19–301.16 (a)(1) (1.16). After withdrawal the attorney is required to refrain from making disclosure of the client's confidences, except as otherwise provided in Rule 19–301.6 (1.6) or in other Rules.

[13] If the attorney knows that despite the withdrawal the client is continuing in conduct that is criminal or fraudulent, and is making use of the fact that the attorney was involved in the matter, the attorney may have to take positive steps to avoid being held to have assisted the conduct. See Rules 19–301.2 (d) (1.2) and 19–304.1 (b) (4.1). In other situations not involving such assistance, the attorney has discretion to make disclosure of otherwise confidential information only in accordance with Rules 19–301.6 (1.6) and 19–301.13 (c) (1.13). Neither this Rule nor Rule 19–301.8 (b) (1.8) nor Rule 19–301.16 (d) (1.16) prevents the attorney from giving notice of the fact of withdrawal, and the attorney may also withdraw or disaffirm any opinion, document, affirmation, or the like.

Dispute Concerning Attorney's Conduct

[14] Where a legal claim or disciplinary charge alleges complicity of the attorney in a client's conduct or other misconduct of the attorney involving representation of the client, the attorney may respond to the extent the attorney reasonably believes necessary to establish a defense. The same is true with respect to a claim involving the conduct or representation of a former client. Such a charge can arise in a civil, criminal, disciplinary or other proceeding and can be based on a wrong allegedly committed by the attorney against the client or on a wrong alleged by a third person, for example, a person claiming to have been defrauded by the attorney and client acting together. The attorney's right to respond arises when an assertion of such complicity has been made. Subsection (b)(5) of this Rule does not require the attorney to await the commencement of an action or proceeding that charges such complicity, so that the defense may be established by responding directly to a third party who has made such an assertion. The right to defend also applies, of course, where a proceeding has been commenced.

[15] An attorney entitled to a fee is permitted by subsection (b)(5) of this Rule to prove the services rendered in an action to collect it. This aspect of the rule expresses the principle that the beneficiary of a fiduciary relationship may not exploit it to the detriment of the fiduciary.

Disclosures Otherwise Required or Authorized

[16] As noted in Comment 7, Rules 19–303.3 (b) (3.3) and 19–304.1 (b) (4.1) require disclosure in some circumstances regardless of whether the disclosure is permitted by Rule 19–301.6 (1.6). Circumstances may be such that disclosure is required under other Rules, for example, Rule 19–301.2 (d) (1.2), in order to avoid assisting a client to perpetrate a crime or fraud.

[17] Other law may require that an attorney disclose information about a client. Whether such a law supersedes Rule 19–301.6 (1.6) is a question of law beyond the scope of these Rules. When disclosure of information relating to the representation appears to be required by other law, the attorney must discuss the matter with the client to

the extent required by Rule 19–301.4 (1.4). If, however, the other law supersedes this Rule and requires disclosure, subsection (b)(6) of this Rule permits the attorney to make such disclosures as are necessary to comply with the law.

[18] An attorney may be ordered to reveal information relating to the representation of a client by a court or by another tribunal or governmental entity claiming authority pursuant to other law to compel the disclosure. Absent informed consent of the client to do otherwise, the attorney should assert on behalf of the client all nonfrivolous claims that the order is not authorized by other law or that the information sought is protected against disclosure by the attorney-client privilege or other applicable law. In the event of an adverse ruling, the attorney must consult with the client about the possibility of appeal to the extent required by Rule 19–301.4 (1.4). Unless review is sought, however, subsection (b)(6) of this Rule permits the attorney to comply with the court's order.

Acting Competently to Preserve Confidentiality

[19] An attorney must act competently to safeguard information relating to the representation of a client against inadvertent or unauthorized disclosure by the attorney or other persons who are participating in the representation of the client or who are subject to the attorney's supervision. See Rules 19–301.1 (1.1), 19–305.1 (5.1) and 19–305.3 (5.3).

[20] When transmitting a communication that includes information relating to the representation of a client, the attorney must take reasonable precautions to prevent the information from coming into the hands of unintended recipients. This duty, however, does not require that the attorney use special security measures if the method of communication affords a reasonable expectation of privacy. Special circumstances, however, may warrant special precautions. Factors to be considered in determining the reasonableness of the attorney's expectation of confidentiality include the sensitivity of the information and the extent to which the privacy of the communication is protected by law or by a confidentiality agreement. A client may require the attorney to implement special

security measures not required by this Rule or may give informed consent to the use of a means of communication that would otherwise be prohibited by this Rule.

Former Client

[21] The duty of confidentiality continues after the client-attorney relationship has terminated. See Rule 19–301.9 (c)(2) (1.9). See Rule 19–301.9 (c)(1) (1.9) for the prohibition against using such information to the disadvantage of the former client.

♦ ♦ ♦

Model Rules Comparison: Rule 19–301.6 (1.6) retains elements of former Rule 1.6 language, incorporates some changes from the Ethics 2000 Amendments to the ABA Model Rules, and incorporates further revisions.

RULE 1.7

Conflict of Interest—General Rule

(a) Except as provided in section (b) of this Rule, an attorney shall not represent a client if the representation involves a conflict of interest. A conflict of interest exists if:

(1) the representation of one client will be directly adverse to another client; or

(2) there is a significant risk that the representation of one or more clients will be materially limited by the attorney's responsibilities to another client, a former client or a third person or by a personal interest of the attorney.

(b) Notwithstanding the existence of a conflict of interest under section (a) of this Rule, an attorney may represent a client if:

(1) the attorney reasonably believes that the attorney will be able to provide competent and diligent representation to each affected client;

(2) the representation is not prohibited by law;

(3) the representation does not involve the assertion of a claim by one client against another client represented by the attorney in the same litigation or other proceeding before a tribunal; and

(4) each affected client gives informed consent, confirmed in writing.

COMMENT

General Principles

[1] Loyalty and independent judgment are essential elements in the attorney's relationship to a client. Conflicts of interest can arise from the attorney's responsibilities to another client, a former client or a third person or from the attorney's own interests. For specific Rules regarding certain conflicts of interest, see Rule 19–301.8 (1.8). For former client conflicts of interest, see Rule 19–301.9 (1.9). For conflicts of interest involving prospective clients, see Rule 19–301.18 (1.18). For definitions of "informed consent" and "confirmed in writing," see Rule 19–301.0 (g) and (b) (1.0).

[2] Resolution of a conflict of interest problem under this Rule requires the attorney to: (1) clearly identify the client or clients; (2) determine whether a conflict of interest exists; (3) decide whether the representation may be undertaken despite the existence of a conflict, i.e., whether the conflict is consentable; and (4) if so, consult with the clients affected under section (a) of this Rule and obtain their informed consent, confirmed in writing. The clients affected under section (a) of this Rule include both of the clients referred to in subsection (a)(1) of this Rule and the one or more clients whose representation might be materially limited under subsection (a)(2) of this Rule.

[3] A conflict of interest may exist before representation is undertaken, in which event the representation must be declined, unless the attorney obtains the informed consent of each client under the conditions of section (b) of this Rule. To determine whether a conflict of interest exists, an attorney should adopt reasonable procedures, appropriate for the size and type of firm and practice, to determine in both litigation and non-litigation matters the persons and issues involved. See also Comment to Rule 19–305.1 (5.1). Ignorance caused by a failure to institute such procedures will not excuse an attorney's violation of this Rule. As to whether a client-attorney

relationship exists or, having once been established, is continuing, see Comment to Rule 19–301.3 (1.3) and Scope.

[4] If a conflict arises after representation has been undertaken, the attorney ordinarily must withdraw from the representation, unless the attorney has obtained the informed consent of the client under the conditions of section (b) of this Rule. See Rule 19–301.16 (1.16). Where more than one client is involved, whether the attorney may continue to represent any of the clients is determined both by the attorney's ability to comply with duties owed to the former client and by the attorney's ability to represent adequately the remaining client or clients, given the attorney's duties to the former client. See Rule 19–301.9 (1.9). See also Comments [5] and [29].

[5] Unforeseeable developments, such as changes in corporate and other organizational affiliations or the addition or realignment of parties in litigation, might create apparent conflicts in the midst of a representation, as when a company sued by the attorney on behalf of one client is bought by another client represented by the attorney in an unrelated matter. Depending on the circumstances, the attorney may have the option to withdraw from one of the representations in order to avoid a conflict under section (a) of this Rule, but the attorney may avoid withdrawal from the affected matter, if and only if each conflicted client provides a signed waiver of conflict after having been provided informed consent confirmed in writing. The attorney must seek court approval where necessary and take steps to minimize harm to the clients. See Rule 19–301.16 (1.16). The attorney must continue to protect the confidences of the client from whose representation the attorney has withdrawn. See Rule 19–301.9 (c) (1.9).

Identifying Conflicts of Interest: Directly Adverse

[6] Loyalty to a current client prohibits undertaking representation directly adverse to that client without that client's informed consent. Thus, absent consent, an attorney may not act as an advocate in one matter against a person the attorney represents in some other matter, even when the matters are wholly unrelated. The client as

to whom the representation is directly adverse is likely to feel betrayed, and the resulting damage to the client-attorney relationship is likely to impair the attorney's ability to represent the client effectively. In addition, the client on whose behalf the adverse representation is undertaken reasonably may fear that the attorney will pursue that client's case less effectively out of deference to the other client, i.e., that the representation may be materially limited by the attorney's interest in retaining the current client. Similarly, a directly adverse conflict may arise when an attorney is required to cross-examine a client who appears as a witness in a lawsuit involving another client, as when the testimony will be damaging to the client who is represented in the lawsuit. On the other hand, simultaneous representation in unrelated matters of clients whose interests are only economically adverse, such as representation of competing economic enterprises in unrelated litigation, does not ordinarily constitute a conflict of interest and thus may not require consent of the respective clients.

[7] Directly adverse conflicts can also arise in transactional matters. For example, if an attorney is asked to represent the seller of a business in negotiations with a buyer represented by the attorney, not in the same transaction but in another, unrelated matter, the attorney could not undertake the representation without the informed consent of each client.

Identifying Conflicts of Interest: Material Limitation

[8] Even where there is no direct adverseness, a conflict of interest exists if there is a significant risk that an attorney's ability to consider, recommend or carry out an appropriate course of action for the client will be materially limited as a result of the attorney's other responsibilities or interests. For example, an attorney asked to represent several individuals seeking to form a joint venture is likely to be materially limited in the attorney's ability to recommend or advocate all possible positions that each might take because of the attorney's duty of loyalty to the others. The conflict in effect forecloses alternatives that would otherwise be available to the client. The mere possibility of subsequent harm does

not itself require disclosure and consent. The critical questions are the likelihood that a difference in interests will eventuate and, if it does, whether it will materially interfere with the attorney's independent professional judgment in considering alternatives or foreclose courses of action that reasonably should be pursued on behalf of the client.

Attorney's Responsibilities to Former Clients and Other Third Persons

[9] In addition to conflicts with other current clients, an attorney's duties of loyalty and independence may be materially limited by responsibilities to former clients under Rule 19–301.9 (1.9) or by the attorney's responsibilities to other persons, such as fiduciary duties arising from an attorney's service as a trustee, executor or corporate director.

Personal Interest Conflicts

[10] The attorney's own interests should not be permitted to have an adverse effect on representation of a client. For example, if the probity of an attorney's own conduct in a transaction is in serious question, it may be difficult or impossible for the attorney to give a client detached advice. Similarly, when an attorney has discussions concerning possible employment with an opponent of the attorney's client, or with a law firm representing the opponent, such discussions could materially limit the attorney's representation of the client. In addition, an attorney may not allow related business interests to affect representation, for example, by referring clients to an enterprise in which the attorney has an undisclosed financial interest. See Rule 19–301.8 (1.8) for specific Rules pertaining to a number of personal interest conflicts, including business transactions with clients. See also Rule 19–301.10 (1.10) (personal interest conflicts under Rule 19–301.7 (1.7) ordinarily are not imputed to other attorneys in a law firm).

[11] When attorneys representing different clients in the same matter or in substantially related matters are closely related by blood or marriage, there may be a significant risk that client confidences

will be revealed and that the attorney's family relationship will interfere with both loyalty and independent professional judgment. As a result, each client is entitled to know of the existence and implications of the relationship between the attorneys before the attorney agrees to undertake the representation. Thus, an attorney related to another attorney, e.g., as parent, child, sibling or spouse, ordinarily may not represent a client in a matter where that attorney is representing another party, unless each client gives informed consent. The disqualification arising from a close family relationship is personal and ordinarily is not imputed to members of firms with whom the attorneys are associated. See Rule 19–301.10 (1.10).

[12] A sexual relationship with a client, whether or not in violation of criminal law, will create an impermissible conflict between the interests of the client and those of the attorney if (1) the representation of the client would be materially limited by the sexual relationship and (2) it is unreasonable for the attorney to believe the attorney can provide competent and diligent representation. Under those circumstances, informed consent by the client is ineffective. See also Rule 19–308.4 (8.4).

Interest of Person Paying for an Attorney's Service

[13] An attorney may be paid from a source other than the client, including a co-client, if the client is informed of that fact and consents and the arrangement does not compromise the attorney's duty of loyalty or independent judgment to the client. See Rule 19–301.8 (f) (1.8). If acceptance of the payment from any other source presents a significant risk that the attorney's representation of the client will be materially limited by the attorney's own interest in accommodating the person paying the attorney's fee or by the attorney's responsibilities to a payer who is also a co-client, then the attorney must comply with the requirements of section (b) of this Rule before accepting the representation, including determining whether the conflict is consentable and, if so, that the client has adequate information about the material risks of the representation.

Prohibited Representations

[14] Ordinarily, clients may consent to representation notwithstanding a conflict. However, as indicated in section (b) of this Rule, some conflicts are nonconsentable, meaning that the attorney involved cannot properly ask for such agreement or provide representation on the basis of the client's consent. When the attorney is representing more than one client, the question of consentability must be resolved as to each client.

[15] Consentability is typically determined by considering whether the interests of the clients will be adequately protected if the clients are permitted to give their informed consent to representation burdened by a conflict of interest. Thus, under subsection (b)(1) of this Rule, representation is prohibited if in the circumstances the attorney cannot reasonably conclude that the attorney will be able to provide competent and diligent representation. See Rule 19–301.1 (1.1) (Competence) and Rule 19–301.3 (1.3) (Diligence).

[16] Subsection (b)(2) of this Rule describes conflicts that are nonconsentable because the representation is prohibited by applicable law. For example, in some states substantive law provides that the same attorney may not represent more than one defendant in a capital case, even with the consent of the clients, and under federal criminal statutes certain representations by a former government attorney are prohibited, despite the informed consent of the former client. In addition, decisional law in some states limits the ability of a governmental client, such as a municipality, to consent to a conflict of interest.

[17] Subsection (b)(3) of this Rule describes conflicts that are nonconsentable because of the institutional interest in vigorous development of each client's position when the clients are aligned directly against each other in the same litigation or other proceeding before a tribunal. Whether clients are aligned directly against each other within the meaning of this subsection requires examination of the context of the proceeding. Although this subsection does not preclude an attorney's multiple representation of adverse parties to a mediation (because mediation is not a proceeding before a

"tribunal" under Rule 19–301.0(p) (1.0)), such representation may be precluded by subsection (b)(1) of this Rule.

Informed Consent

[18] Informed consent requires that each affected client be aware of the relevant circumstances and of the material and reasonably foreseeable ways that the conflict could have adverse effects on the interests of that client. See Rule 19–301.0 (g) (1.0) (informed consent). The information required depends on the nature of the conflict and the nature of the risks involved. When representation of multiple clients in a single matter is undertaken, the information must include the implications of the common representation, including possible effects on loyalty, confidentiality and the attorney-client privilege and the advantages and risks involved. See Comments [30] and [31] (effect of common representation on confidentiality).

[19] Under some circumstances it may be impossible to make the disclosure necessary to obtain consent. For example, when the attorney represents different clients in related matters and one of the clients refuses to consent to the disclosure necessary to permit the other client to make an informed decision, the attorney cannot properly ask the latter to consent. In some cases the alternative to common representation can be that each party may have to obtain separate representation with the possibility of incurring additional costs. These costs, along with the benefits of securing separate representation, are factors that may be considered by the affected client in determining whether common representation is in the client's interests.

Consent Confirmed in Writing

[20] Section (b) of this Rule requires the attorney to obtain the informed consent of the client, confirmed in writing. Such a writing may consist of a document executed by the client or one that the attorney promptly records and transmits to the client following an oral consent. See Rule 19–301.0 (b) (1.0). See also Rule 19–301.0 (q) (1.0) (writing includes electronic transmission). If it is not feasible to obtain or transmit the writing at the time the client gives informed

consent, then the attorney must obtain or transmit it within a reasonable time thereafter. See Rule 19–301.0 (b) (1.0). The requirement of a writing does not supplant the need in most cases for the attorney to talk with the client, to explain the risks and advantages, if any, of representation burdened with a conflict of interest, as well as reasonably available alternatives, and to afford the client a reasonable opportunity to consider the risks and alternatives and to raise questions and concerns. Rather, the writing is required in order to impress upon clients the seriousness of the decision the client is being asked to make and to avoid disputes or ambiguities that might later occur in the absence of a writing.

Revoking Consent

[21] A client who has given consent to a conflict may revoke the consent and, like any other client, may terminate the attorney's representation at any time. Whether revoking consent to the client's own representation precludes the attorney from continuing to represent other clients depends on the circumstances, including the nature of the conflict, whether the client revoked consent because of a material change in circumstances, the reasonable expectations of the other client and whether material detriment to the other clients or the attorney would result.

Consent to Future Conflict

[22] Whether an attorney may properly request a client to waive conflicts that might arise in the future is subject to the test of section (b) of this Rule. The effectiveness of such waivers is generally determined by the extent to which the client reasonably understands the material risks that the waiver entails. The more comprehensive the explanation of the types of future representations that might arise and the actual and reasonably foreseeable adverse consequences of those representations, the greater the likelihood that the client will have the requisite understanding. Thus, if the client agrees to consent to a particular type of conflict with which the client is already familiar, then the consent ordinarily will be effective with regard to that type of conflict. If the consent is general

and open-ended, then the consent ordinarily will be ineffective, because it is not reasonably likely that the client will have understood the material risks involved. On the other hand, if the client is an experienced user of the legal services involved and is reasonably informed regarding the risk that a conflict may arise, such consent is more likely to be effective, particularly if, e.g., the client is independently represented by another attorney in giving consent and the consent is limited to future conflicts unrelated to the subject of the representation. In any case, advance consent cannot be effective if the circumstances that materialize in the future are such as would make the conflict nonconsentable under section (b).

Conflicts in Litigation

[23] Subsection (b)(3) of this Rule prohibits representation of opposing parties in the same litigation, regardless of the clients' consent. On the other hand, simultaneous representation of parties whose interests in litigation may conflict, such as coplaintiffs or codefendants, is governed by subsection (a)(2) of this Rule. A conflict may exist by reason of substantial discrepancy in the parties' testimony, incompatibility in positions in relation to an opposing party or the fact that there are substantially different possibilities of settlement of the claims or liabilities in question. Such conflicts can arise in criminal cases as well as civil. The potential for conflict of interest in representing multiple defendants in a criminal case is so grave that ordinarily an attorney should decline to represent more than one codefendant. On the other hand, common representation of persons having similar interests in civil litigation is proper if the requirements of section (b) of this Rule are met.

[24] Ordinarily an attorney may take inconsistent legal positions in different tribunals at different times on behalf of different clients. The mere fact that advocating a legal position on behalf of one client might create precedent adverse to the interests of a client represented by the attorney in an unrelated matter does not create a conflict of interest. A conflict of interest exists, however, if there is a significant risk that an attorney's action on behalf of one client will materially limit the attorney's effectiveness in representing

another client in a different case; for example, when a decision favoring one client will create a precedent likely to seriously weaken the position taken on behalf of the other client. Factors relevant in determining whether the clients need to be advised of the risk include: where the cases are pending, whether the issue is substantive or procedural, the temporal relationship between the matters, the significance of the issue to the immediate and long-term interests of the clients involved and the clients' reasonable expectations in retaining the attorney. If there is significant risk of material limitation, then absent informed consent of the affected clients, the attorney must refuse one of the representations or withdraw from one or both matters.

[25] When an attorney represents or seeks to represent a class of plaintiffs or defendants in a class-action lawsuit, unnamed members of the class are ordinarily not considered to be clients of the attorney for purposes of applying subsection (a)(1) of this Rule. Thus, the attorney does not typically need to get the consent of such a person before representing a client suing the person in an unrelated matter. Similarly, an attorney seeking to represent an opponent in a class action does not typically need the consent of an unnamed member of the class whom the attorney represents in an unrelated matter.

Nonlitigation Conflicts

[26] Conflicts of interest under subsections (a)(1) and (a)(2) of this Rule arise in contexts other than litigation. For a discussion of directly adverse conflicts in transactional matters, see Comment [7]. Relevant factors in determining whether there is significant potential for material limitation include the duration and intimacy of the attorney's relationship with the client or clients involved, the functions being performed by the attorney, the likelihood that disagreements will arise and the likely prejudice to the client from the conflict. The question is often one of proximity and degree. See Comment [8].

[27] For example, conflict questions may arise in estate planning and estate administration. An attorney may be called upon to prepare wills for several family members, such as husband and wife, and,

depending upon the circumstances, a conflict of interest may be present. In estate administration the identity of the client may be unclear under the law of a particular jurisdiction. Under one view, the client is the fiduciary; under another view the client is the estate or trust, including its beneficiaries. In order to comply with conflict of interest rules, the attorney should make clear the attorney's relationship to the parties involved.

[28] Whether a conflict is consentable depends on the circumstances. For example, an attorney may not represent multiple parties to a negotiation whose interests are fundamentally antagonistic to each other, but common representation is permissible where the clients are generally aligned in interest even though there is some difference in interest among them. Thus, an attorney may seek to establish or adjust a relationship between clients on an amicable and mutually advantageous basis; for example, in helping to organize a business in which two or more clients are entrepreneurs, working out the financial reorganization of an enterprise in which two or more clients have an interest or arranging a property distribution in settlement of an estate. The attorney seeks to resolve potentially adverse interests by developing the parties' mutual interests. Otherwise, each party might have to obtain separate representation, with the possibility of incurring additional cost, complication or even litigation. Given these and other relevant factors, the clients may prefer that the attorney act for all of them.

Special Considerations in Common Representation

[29] In considering whether to represent multiple clients in the same matter, an attorney should be mindful that if the common representation fails because the potentially adverse interests cannot be reconciled, the result can be additional cost, embarrassment and recrimination. Ordinarily, the attorney will be forced to withdraw from representing all of the clients if the common representation fails. In some situations, the risk of failure is so great that multiple representation is plainly impossible. For example, an attorney cannot undertake common representation of clients where contentious litigation or negotiations between them are imminent

or contemplated. Moreover, because the attorney is required to be impartial between commonly represented clients, representation of multiple clients is improper when it is unlikely that impartiality can be maintained. Generally, if the relationship between the parties has already assumed antagonism, the possibility that the clients' interests can be adequately served by common representation is not very good. Other relevant factors are whether the attorney subsequently will represent both parties on a continuing basis and whether the situation involves creating or terminating a relationship between the parties.

[29.1] Rule 19–301.7 (1.7) may not apply to an attorney appointed by a court to serve as a Child's Best Interest Attorney in the same way that it applies to other attorneys. For example, because the Child's Best Interest Attorney is not bound to advocate a client's objective, siblings with conflicting views may not pose a conflict of interest for a Child's Best Interest Attorney, provided that the attorney determines the siblings' best interests to be consistent. A Child's Best Interest Attorney should advocate for the children's best interests and ensure that each child's position is made a part of the record, even if that position is different from the position that the attorney advocates. See Md. Rule 9–205.1 and Appendix to the Maryland Rules: Maryland Guidelines for Practice for Court-appointed Attorneys Representing Children in Cases Involving Child Custody or Child Access.

[30] A particularly important factor in determining the appropriateness of common representation is the effect on client-attorney confidentiality and the attorney-client privilege. With regard to the attorney-client privilege, the prevailing rule is that, as between commonly represented clients, the privilege does not attach. Hence, it must be assumed that if litigation eventuates between the clients, the privilege will not protect any such communications, and the clients should be so advised.

[31] As to the duty of confidentiality, continued common representation will almost certainly be inadequate if one client asks the attorney not to disclose to the other client information relevant to the common representation. This is so because the attorney has an equal

duty of loyalty to each client, and each client has the right to be informed of anything bearing on the representation that might affect that client's interests and the right to expect that the attorney will use that information to that client's benefit. See Rule 19–301.4 (1.4). The attorney should, at the outset of the common representation and as part of the process of obtaining each client's informed consent, advise each client that information will be shared and that the attorney will have to withdraw if one client decides that some matter material to the representation should be kept from the other. In limited circumstances, it may be appropriate for the attorney to proceed with the representation when the clients have agreed, after being properly informed, that the attorney will keep certain information confidential. For example, the attorney may reasonably conclude that failure to disclose one client's trade secrets to another client will not adversely affect representation involving a joint venture between the clients and agree to keep that information confidential with the informed consent of both clients.

[32] When seeking to establish or adjust a relationship between clients, the attorney should make clear that the attorney's role is not that of partisanship normally expected in other circumstances and, thus, that the clients may be required to assume greater responsibility for decisions than when each client is separately represented. Any limitations on the scope of the representation made necessary as a result of the common representation should be fully explained to the clients at the outset of the representation. See Rule 19–301.2 (c) (1.2).

[33] Subject to the above limitations, each client in the common representation has the right to loyal and diligent representation and the protection of Rule 19–301.9 (1.9) concerning the obligations to a former client. The client also has the right to discharge the attorney as stated in Rule 19–301.16 (1.16).

Organizational Clients

[34] An attorney who represents a corporation or other organization does not, by virtue of that representation, necessarily represent any constituent or affiliated organization, such as a parent

or subsidiary. See Rule 19–301.13(a) (1.13). Thus, the attorney for an organization is not barred from accepting representation adverse to an affiliate in an unrelated matter, unless the circumstances are such that the affiliate should also be considered a client of the attorney, there is an understanding between the attorney and the organizational client that the attorney will avoid representation adverse to the client's affiliates, or the attorney's obligations to either the organizational client or the new client are likely to limit materially the attorney's representation of the other client.

[35] An attorney for a corporation or other organization who is also a member of its board of directors should determine whether the responsibilities of the two roles may conflict. The attorney may be called on to advise the corporation in matters involving actions of the directors. Consideration should be given to the frequency with which such situations may arise, the potential intensity of the conflict, the effect of the attorney's resignation from the board and the possibility of the corporation's obtaining legal advice from another attorney in such situations. If there is material risk that the dual role will compromise the attorney's independence of professional judgment, the attorney should not serve as a director or should cease to act as the corporation's attorney when conflicts of interest arise. The attorney should advise the other members of the board that in some circumstances matters discussed at board meetings while the attorney is present in the capacity of director might not be protected by the attorney-client privilege and that conflict of interest considerations might require the attorney's recusal as a director or might require the attorney and the attorney's firm to decline representation of the corporation in a matter.

♦ ♦ ♦

Model Rules Comparison: Rule 19–301.7 (1.7) is substantially similar to the language of the Ethics 2000 Amendments to the ABA Model Rules of Professional Conduct except for omitting the word "concurrent" in Rule 19–301.7 (1.7) (a) and (b) and Comment [1], adding language to Comment [5], and retaining most of existing Maryland language in Comment [12].

RULE 1.8

CONFLICT OF INTEREST: CURRENT CLIENTS: SPECIFIC RULES

(a) An attorney shall not enter into a business transaction with a client unless:

(1) the transaction and terms on which the attorney acquires the interest are fair and reasonable to the client and are fully disclosed and transmitted in writing in a manner that can be reasonably understood by the client;

(2) the client is advised in writing of the desirability of seeking and is given a reasonable opportunity to seek independent legal advice on the transaction; and

(3) the client gives informed consent, in a writing signed by the client, to the essential terms of the transaction and the attorney's role in the transaction, including whether the attorney is representing the client in the transaction.

(b) An attorney shall not use information relating to representation of a client to the disadvantage of the client unless the client gives informed consent, except as permitted or required by these Rules.

(c) An attorney shall not solicit any substantial gift from a client, including a testamentary gift, or prepare on behalf of a client an instrument giving the attorney or a person related to the attorney any substantial gift unless the attorney or other recipient of the gift is related to the client. For purposes of this section, related persons include a spouse, child, grandchild, parent, grandparent or other relative or individual with whom the attorney or the client maintains a close, familial relationship.

(d) Prior to the conclusion of representation of a client, an attorney shall not make or negotiate an agreement giving the attorney literary or media rights to a portrayal or account based in substantial part on information relating to the representation.

(e) An attorney shall not provide financial assistance to a client in connection with pending or contemplated litigation, except that:

(1) an attorney may advance court costs and expenses of litigation, the repayment of which may be contingent on the outcome of the matter; and

(2) an attorney representing an indigent client may pay court costs and expenses of litigation on behalf of the client.

(f) An attorney shall not accept compensation for representing a client from one other than the client unless:

(1) the client gives informed consent;

(2) there is no interference with the attorney's independence of professional judgment or with the client-attorney relationship; and

(3) information relating to representation of a client is protected as required by Rule 19–301.6 (1.6).

(g) An attorney who represents two or more clients shall not participate in making an aggregate settlement of the claims of or against the clients, or in a criminal case an aggregated agreement as to guilty or nolo contendere pleas, unless each client gives informed consent, in a writing signed by the client or confirmed on the record before a tribunal. The attorney's disclosure shall include the existence and nature of all the claims or pleas involved and of the participation of each person in the settlement.

(h) An attorney shall not:

(1) make an agreement prospectively limiting the attorney's liability to a client for malpractice unless the client is independently represented in making the agreement; or

(2) settle a claim or potential claim for such liability with an unrepresented client or former client unless that person is advised in writing of the desirability of seeking and is given a reasonable opportunity to seek independent legal advice in connection therewith.

(i) An attorney shall not acquire a proprietary interest in the cause of action or subject matter of litigation the attorney is conducting for a client, except that the attorney may:

(1) acquire a lien authorized by law to secure the attorney's fee or expenses; and

(2) subject to Rule 19–301.5 (1.5), contract with a client for a reasonable contingent fee in a civil case.

(j) While attorneys are associated in a firm, a prohibition in the foregoing sections (a) through (i) of this Rule that applies to any one of them shall apply to all of them.

COMMENT

Business Transactions Between Client and Attorney

[1] An attorney's legal skill and training, together with the relationship of trust and confidence between attorney and client, create the possibility of overreaching when the attorney participates in a business, property or financial transaction with a client, for example, a loan or sales transaction or an attorney investment on behalf of a client. The requirements of section (a) of this Rule must be met even when the transaction is not closely related to the subject matter of the representation, as when an attorney drafting a will for a client learns that the client needs money for unrelated expenses and offers to make a loan to the client. Section (a) of this Rule also applies to attorneys purchasing property from estates they represent. It does not apply to ordinary fee arrangements between client and attorney, which are governed by Rule 19–301.5 (1.5), although its requirements must be met when the attorney accepts an interest in the client's business or other nonmonetary property as payment of all or part of a fee. In addition, the Rule does not apply to standard commercial transactions between the attorney and the client for products or services that the client generally markets to others, for example, banking or brokerage services, medical services, products manufactured or distributed by the client, and utilities' services. In such transactions, the attorney has no advantage in dealing with the client, and the restrictions in section (a) of this Rule are unnecessary and impracticable. For restrictions regarding attorneys engaged in the sale of goods or services related to the practice of law, see Rule 19–305.7 (5.7).

[2] Subsection (a)(1) of this Rule requires that the transaction itself be fair to the client and that its essential terms be communicated to the client, in writing, in a manner that can be reasonably understood. Subsection (a)(2) of this Rule requires that the client also be advised, in writing, of the desirability of seeking independent legal advice. It also requires that the client be given a reasonable opportunity to obtain such advice. Subsection (a)(3) of this Rule requires that the attorney obtain the client's informed consent, in a writing signed by the client, both to the essential terms of the transaction and to the attorney's role. When necessary, the attorney should discuss both the material risks of the proposed transaction, including any risk presented by the attorney's involvement, and the existence of reasonably available alternatives and should explain why independent legal advice is desirable. See Rule 19–301.0 (g) (1.0) (definition of informed consent).

[3] The risk to a client is greatest when the client expects the attorney to represent the client in the transaction itself or when the attorney's financial interest otherwise poses a significant risk that the attorney's representation of the client will be materially limited by the attorney's financial interest in the transaction. Here the attorney's role requires that the attorney must comply, not only with the requirements of section (a) of this Rule, but also with the requirements of Rule 19–301.7 (1.7). Under that Rule, the attorney must disclose the risks associated with the attorney's dual role as both legal adviser and participant in the transaction, such as the risk that the attorney will structure the transaction or give legal advice in a way that favors the attorney's interests at the expense of the client. Moreover, the attorney must obtain the client's informed consent. In some cases, the attorney's interest may be such that Rule 19–301.7 (1.7) will preclude the attorney from seeking the client's consent to the transaction.

[4] If the client is independently represented in the transaction, subsection (a)(2) of this Rule is inapplicable, and the subsection (a)(1) of this Rule requirement for full disclosure is satisfied either by a written disclosure by the attorney involved in the transaction or by

the client's independent attorney. The fact that the client was independently represented in the transaction is relevant in determining whether the agreement was fair and reasonable to the client as subsection (a)(1) of this Rule further requires.

Use of Information Related to Representation

[5] Use of information relating to the representation to the disadvantage of the client violates the attorney's duty of loyalty. Section (b) of this Rule applies when the information is used to benefit either the attorney or a third person, such as another client or business associate of the attorney. For example, if an attorney learns that a client intends to purchase and develop several parcels of land, the attorney may not use that information to purchase one of the parcels in competition with the client or to recommend that another client make such a purchase. The Rule does not prohibit uses that do not disadvantage the client. For example, an attorney who learns a government agency's interpretation of trade legislation during the representation of one client may properly use that information to benefit other clients. Section (b) of this Rule prohibits disadvantageous use of client information unless the client gives informed consent, except as permitted or required by these Rules. See Rules 19–301.2 (d) (1.2), 19–301.6 (1.6), 19–301.9 (c) (1.9), 19–303.3 (3.3), 19–304.1 (b) (4.1), 19–308.1 (8.1) and 19–308.3 (8.3).

Gifts to Attorneys

[6] An attorney may accept a gift from a client, if the transaction meets general standards of fairness. For example, a simple gift such as a present given at a holiday or as a token of appreciation is permitted. If a client offers the attorney a more substantial gift, section (c) of this Rule does not prohibit the attorney from accepting it, although such a gift may be voidable by the client under the doctrine of undue influence, which treats client gifts as presumptively fraudulent. In any event, due to concerns about overreaching and imposition on clients, an attorney may not suggest that a substantial gift be made to the attorney or for the attorney's benefit, except

where the attorney is related to the client as set forth in section (c) of this Rule.

[7] If effectuation of a substantial gift requires preparing a legal instrument such as a will or conveyance, the client should have the detached advice that another attorney can provide. The sole exception to this Rule is where the client is a relative of the donee.

[8] This Rule does not prohibit an attorney from seeking to have the attorney or a partner or associate of the attorney named as executor of the client's estate or to another potentially lucrative fiduciary position. Nevertheless, such appointments will be subject to the general conflict of interest provision in Rule 19–301.7 (1.7) when there is a significant risk that the attorney's interest in obtaining the appointment will materially limit the attorney's independent professional judgment in advising the client concerning the choice of an executor or other fiduciary. In obtaining the client's informed consent to the conflict, the attorney should advise the client concerning the nature and extent of the attorney's financial interest in the appointment, as well as the availability of alternative candidates for the position.

Literary Rights

[9] An agreement by which an attorney acquires literary or media rights concerning the conduct of the representation creates a conflict between the interests of the client and the personal interests of the attorney. Measures suitable in the representation of the client may detract from the publication value of an account of the representation. Section (d) of this Rule does not prohibit an attorney representing a client in a transaction concerning literary property from agreeing that the attorney's fee shall consist of a share in ownership in the property, if the arrangement conforms to Rule 19–301.5 (1.5) and sections (a) and (i) of this Rule.

Financial Assistance

[10] Attorneys may not subsidize lawsuits or administrative proceedings brought on behalf of their clients, including making or guaranteeing loans to their clients for living expenses, because to do so

would encourage clients to pursue lawsuits that might not otherwise be brought and because such assistance gives attorneys too great a financial stake in the litigation. These dangers do not warrant a prohibition on an attorney lending a client court costs and litigation expenses, including the expenses of medical examination and the costs of obtaining and presenting evidence, because these advances are virtually indistinguishable from contingent fees and help ensure access to the courts. Similarly, an exception allowing attorneys representing indigent clients to pay court costs and litigation expenses regardless of whether these funds will be repaid is warranted.

Person Paying for an Attorney's Services

[11] Attorneys are frequently asked to represent a client under circumstances in which a third person will compensate the attorney, in whole or in part. The third person might be a relative or friend, an indemnitor (such as a liability insurance company) or a co-client (such as a corporation sued along with one or more of its employees). Because third-party payers frequently have interests that differ from those of the client, including interests in minimizing the amount spent on the representation and in learning how the representation is progressing, attorneys are prohibited from accepting or continuing such representations unless the attorney determines that there will be no interference with the attorney's independent professional judgment and there is informed consent from the client. See also Rule 19–305.4 (c) (5.4) (prohibiting interference with a attorney's professional judgment by one who recommends, employs or pays the attorney to render legal services for another).

[12] Sometimes, it will be sufficient for the attorney to obtain the client's informed consent regarding the fact of the payment and the identity of the third-party payer. If, however, the fee arrangement creates a conflict of interest for the attorney, then the attorney must comply with Rule 19–301.7 (1.7). The attorney must also conform to the requirements of Rule 19–301.6 (1.6) concerning confidentiality. Under Rule 19–301.7 (a) (1.7), a conflict of interest exists if there is significant risk that the attorney's representation of the

client will be materially limited by the attorney's own interest in the fee arrangement or by the attorney's responsibilities to the third-party payer (for example, when the third-party payer is a co-client). Under Rule 19–301.7 (b) (1.7), the attorney may accept or continue the representation with the informed consent of each affected client, unless the conflict is nonconsentable under that section. Under Rule 19–301.7 (b) (1.7), the informed consent must be confirmed in writing.

Aggregate Settlements

[13] Differences in willingness to make or accept an offer of settlement are among the risks of common representation of multiple clients by a single attorney. Under Rule 19–301.7 (1.7), this is one of the risks that should be discussed before undertaking the representation, as part of the process of obtaining the clients' informed consent. In addition, Rule 19–301.2 (a) (1.2) protects each client's right to have the final say in deciding whether to accept or reject an offer of settlement and in deciding whether to enter a guilty or nolo contendere plea in a criminal case. The rule stated in this section is a corollary of both these Rules and provides that, before any settlement offer or plea bargain is made or accepted on behalf of multiple clients, the attorney must inform each of them about all the material terms of the settlement, including what the other clients will receive or pay if the settlement or plea offer is accepted. See also Rule 19–301.0 (g) (1.0) (definition of informed consent). Attorneys representing a class of plaintiffs or defendants, or those proceeding derivatively, may not have a full client-attorney relationship with each member of the class; nevertheless, such attorneys must comply with applicable rules regulating notification of class members and other procedural requirements designed to ensure adequate protection of the entire class.

Limiting Liability and Settling Malpractice Claims

[14] Agreements prospectively limiting an attorney's liability for malpractice are prohibited unless the client is independently represented in making the agreement because they are likely to undermine

competent and diligent representation. Also, many clients are unable to evaluate the desirability of making such an agreement before a dispute has arisen, particularly if they are then represented by the attorney seeking the agreement. This section does not, however, prohibit an attorney from entering into an agreement with the client to arbitrate existing legal malpractice claims, provided the client is fully informed of the scope and effect of the agreement. Nor does this section limit the ability of attorneys to practice in the form of a limited-liability entity, where permitted by law, provided that each attorney remains personally liable to the client for his or her own conduct and the firm complies with any conditions required by law, such as provisions requiring client notification or maintenance of adequate liability insurance. Nor does it prohibit an agreement in accordance with Rule 19–301.2 (1.2) that defines the scope of the representation, although a definition of scope that makes the obligations of representation illusory will amount to an attempt to limit liability.

[15] Agreements settling a claim or a potential claim for malpractice are not prohibited by this Rule. Nevertheless, in view of the danger that an attorney will take unfair advantage of an unrepresented client or former client, the attorney must first advise such a person in writing of the appropriateness of independent representation in connection with such a settlement. In addition, the attorney must give the client or former client a reasonable opportunity to find and consult independent attorney.

Acquiring Proprietary Interest in Litigation

[16] Section (i) of this Rule states the traditional general rule that attorneys are prohibited from acquiring a proprietary interest in litigation. Like section (e) of this Rule, the general rule has its basis in common law champerty and maintenance and is designed to avoid giving the attorney too great an interest in the representation. In addition, when the attorney acquires an ownership interest in the subject of the representation, it will be more difficult for a client to discharge the attorney if the client so desires. The Rule is subject to specific exceptions developed in decisional law

and continued in these Rules. The exception for certain advances of the costs of litigation is set forth in section (e) of this Rule. In addition, section (i) of this Rule sets forth exceptions for liens authorized by law to secure the attorney's fees or expenses and contracts for reasonable contingent fees. The law of each jurisdiction determines which liens are authorized by law. These may include liens granted by statute, liens originating in common law and liens acquired by contract with the client. When an attorney acquires by contract a security interest in property other than that recovered through the attorney's efforts in the litigation, such an acquisition is a business or financial transaction with a client and is governed by the requirements of section (a) of this Rule. Contracts for contingent fees in civil cases are governed by Rule 19–301.5 (1.5).

Imputation of Prohibitions

[17] Under section (i) of this Rule, a prohibition on conduct by an individual attorney in sections (a) through (i) of this Rule also applies to all attorneys associated in a firm with the personally prohibited attorney. For example, one attorney in a firm may not enter into a business transaction with a client of another member of the firm without complying with section (a) of this Rule, even if the first attorney is not personally involved in the representation of the client.

♦ ♦ ♦

Model Rules Comparison: Rule 19–301.8 (1.8) is substantially similar to the language of the Ethics 2000 Amendments to the ABA Model Rules of Professional Conduct, except for wording changes to Rule 19–301.8 (1.8) (a), (g), (i)(2) and Comments [1], [14] and [17], and the omission of Model Rule 1.8 (j) with appropriate redesignation of subsections.

RULE 1.9

DUTIES TO FORMER CLIENTS

(a) An attorney who has formerly represented a client in a matter shall not thereafter represent another person in the same or a substantially related matter in which that person's interests are materially adverse to the interests of the former client unless the former client gives informed consent, confirmed in writing.

(b) An attorney shall not knowingly represent a person in the same or a substantially related matter in which a firm with which the attorney formerly was associated had previously represented a client:

(1) whose interests are materially adverse to that person; and

(2) about whom the attorney had acquired information protected by Rules 19–301.6 (1.6) and 19–301.9 (c) (1.9) that is material to the matter; unless the former client gives informed consent, confirmed in writing.

(c) An attorney who has formerly represented a client in a matter or whose present or former firm has formerly represented a client in a matter shall not thereafter:

(1) use information relating to the representation to the disadvantage of the former client except as these Rules would permit or require with respect to a client, or when the information has become generally known; or

(2) reveal information relating to the representation except as these Rules would permit or require with respect to a client.

COMMENT

[1] After termination of a client-attorney relationship, an attorney has certain continuing duties with respect to confidentiality and conflicts of interest and thus may not represent another client except in conformity with this Rule. Under this Rule, for example, an attorney could not properly seek to rescind on behalf of a new client a contract drafted on behalf of the former client. So also an attorney who has prosecuted an accused person could not properly represent the accused in a subsequent civil action against the government concerning the same transaction. Nor could an attorney who has represented multiple clients in a matter represent one of the clients against the others in the same or a substantially related matter after a dispute arose among the clients in that matter, unless all affected clients give informed consent. See Comment [9]. Current and former government

attorneys must comply with this Rule to the extent required by Rule 19–301.11 (1.11).

[2] The scope of a "matter" for purposes of this Rule depends on the facts of a particular situation or transaction. The attorney's involvement in a matter can also be a question of degree. When an attorney has been directly involved in a specific transaction, subsequent representation of other clients with materially adverse interests in that transaction clearly is prohibited. On the other hand, an attorney who recurrently handled a type of problem for a former client is not precluded for that reason alone from later representing another client in a factually distinct problem of that type even though the subsequent representation involves a position adverse to the prior client. Similar considerations can apply to the reassignment of military attorneys between defense and prosecution functions within the same military jurisdictions. The underlying question is whether the attorney was so involved in the matter that the subsequent representation can be justly regarded as a changing of sides in the matter in question.

[3] Matters are "substantially related" for purposes of this Rule if they involve the same transaction or legal dispute or if there otherwise is a substantial risk that confidential factual information as would normally have been obtained in the prior representation would materially advance the client's position in the subsequent matter. For example, an attorney who has represented a businessperson and learned extensive private financial information about that individual may not then represent that individual's spouse in seeking a divorce. Similarly, an attorney who has previously represented a client in securing environmental permits to build a shopping center would be precluded from representing neighbors seeking to oppose rezoning of the property on the basis of environmental considerations; however, the attorney would not be precluded, on the grounds of substantial relationship, from defending a tenant of the completed shopping center in resisting eviction for nonpayment of rent. Information that has been disclosed to the public or to other parties adverse to the former client ordinarily will not be disqualifying. Information acquired in a prior representation may

have been rendered obsolete by the passage of time, a circumstance that may be relevant in determining whether two representations are substantially related. In the case of an organizational client, general knowledge of the client's policies and practices ordinarily will not preclude a subsequent representation; on the other hand, knowledge of specific facts gained in a prior representation that are relevant to the matter in question ordinarily will preclude such a representation. A former client is not required to reveal the confidential information learned by the attorney in order to establish a substantial risk that the attorney has confidential information to use in the subsequent matter. A conclusion about the possession of such information may be based on the nature of the services the attorney provided the former client and information that would in ordinary practice be learned by an attorney providing such services.

Attorneys Moving Between Firms

[4] When attorneys have been associated within a firm but then end their association, the question of whether an attorney should undertake representation is more complicated. There are several competing considerations. First, the client previously represented by the former firm must be reasonably assured that the principle of loyalty to the client is not compromised. Second, the rule should not be so broadly cast as to preclude other persons from having reasonable choice of attorneys. Third, the rule should not unreasonably hamper attorneys from forming new associations and taking on new clients after having left a previous association. In this connection, it should be recognized that today many attorneys practice in firms, that many attorneys to some degree limit their practice to one field or another, and that many move from one association to another several times in their careers. If the concept of imputation were applied with unqualified rigor, the result would be radical curtailment of the opportunity of attorneys to move from one practice setting to another and of the opportunity of clients to change attorneys.

[5] Section (b) of this Rule operates to disqualify the attorney only when the attorney involved has actual knowledge of information

protected by Rules 19–301.6 (1.6) and 19–301.9 (c) (1.9). Thus, if an attorney while with one firm acquired no knowledge or information relating to a particular client of the firm, and that attorney later joined another firm, neither the attorney individually nor the second firm is disqualified from representing another client in the same or a related matter even though the interests of the two clients conflict. See Rule 19–301.10 (b) (1.10) for the restrictions on a firm once an attorney has terminated association with the firm.

[6] Application of section (b) of this Rule depends on a situation's particular facts, aided by inferences, deductions or working presumptions that reasonably may be made about the way in which attorneys work together. An attorney may have general access to files of all clients of a law firm and may regularly participate in discussions of their affairs; it should be inferred that such an attorney in fact is privy to all information about all the firm's clients. In contrast, another attorney may have access to the files of only a limited number of clients and participate in discussions of the affairs of no other clients; in the absence of information to the contrary, it should be inferred that such an attorney in fact is privy to information about the clients actually served but not those of other clients. In such an inquiry, the burden of proof ordinarily rests upon the firm whose disqualification is sought.

[7] Independent of the question of disqualification of a firm, an attorney changing professional association has a continuing duty to preserve confidentiality of information about a client formerly represented. See Rules 19–301.6 (1.6) and 19–301.9 (c) (1.9).

[8] Section (c) of this Rule provides that information acquired by the attorney in the course of representing a client may not subsequently be used or revealed by the attorney to the disadvantage of the client. However, the fact that an attorney has once served a client does not preclude the attorney from using generally known information about that client when later representing another client.

[9] The provisions of this Rule are for the protection of former clients and can be waived if the client gives informed consent, which consent must be confirmed in writing under sections (a) and (b) of this Rule. See Rule 19–301.0 (g) (1.0). With regard to the effectiveness

of an advance waiver, see Comment [22] to Rule 19–301.7 (1.7). With regard to disqualification of a firm with which an attorney is or was formerly associated, see Rule 19–301.10 (1.10).

♦ ♦ ♦

Model Rules Comparison: Rule 19–301.9 (1.9) is substantially similar to the language of the Ethics 2000 Amendments to the ABA Model Rules of Professional Conduct except for wording changes to Comments [2] and [6].

RULE 1.10

Imputation of Conflicts of Interest—General Rule

(a) While attorneys are associated in a firm, none of them shall knowingly represent a client when any one of them practicing alone would be prohibited from doing so by Rules 19–301.7 (1.7) or 19–301.9 (1.9), unless the prohibition is based on a personal interest of the prohibited attorney and does not present a significant risk of materially limiting the representation of the client by the remaining attorneys in the firm.

(b) When an attorney has terminated an association with a firm, the firm is not prohibited from thereafter representing a person with interests materially adverse to those of a client represented by the formerly associated attorney and not currently represented by the firm, unless:

(1) the matter is the same or substantially related to that in which the formerly associated attorney represented the client; and

(2) any attorney remaining in the firm has information protected by Rules 19–301.6 (1.6) and 19–301.9 (c) (1.9) that is material to the matter.

(c) When an attorney becomes associated with a firm, no attorney associated in the firm shall knowingly represent a person in a matter in which the newly associated attorney is disqualified under Rule 19–301.9 (1.9) unless the personally disqualified attorney is timely screened from any participation in the matter and is apportioned no part of the fee therefrom.

(d) A disqualification prescribed by this Rule may be waived by the affected client under the conditions stated in Rule 19–301.7 (1.7).

(e) The disqualification of attorneys associated in a firm with former or current government attorneys is governed by Rule 19–301.11 (1.11).

COMMENT

Definition of "Firm"

[1] A "firm" is defined in Rule 19–301.0 (e) (1.0). Whether two or more attorneys constitute a firm within this definition can depend on the specific facts. See Rule 19–301.0 (1.0), Comments [3]—[5]. An attorney is deemed associated with a firm if held out to be a partner, principal, associate, of counsel, or similar designation. An attorney ordinarily is not deemed associated with a firm if the attorney no longer practices law and is held out as retired or emeritus. An attorney employed for short periods as a contract attorney ordinarily is deemed associated with the firm only regarding matters to which the attorney gives substantive attention.

Principles of Imputed Disqualification

[2] The rule of imputed disqualification stated in section (a) gives effect to the principle of loyalty to the client as it applies to attorneys who practice in a law firm. Such situations can be considered from the premise that a firm of attorneys is essentially one attorney for purposes of the rules governing loyalty to the client, or from the premise that each attorney is vicariously bound by the obligation of loyalty owed by each attorney with whom the attorney is associated. Section (a) of this Rule operates only among the attorneys currently associated in a firm. When an attorney moves from one firm to another, the situation is governed by Rules 19–301.9 (b) (1.9), 19–301.10 (b) (1.10) and 19–301.10 (c) (1.10).

[3] The rule in section (a) of this Rule does not prohibit representation where neither questions of client loyalty nor protection of confidential information are presented. Where one attorney in a firm could not effectively represent a given client because of strong political beliefs, for example, but that attorney will do no work on the case and the personal beliefs of the attorney will not materially limit the representation by others in the firm, the firm should not be

disqualified. On the other hand, if an opposing party in a case were owned by an attorney in the law firm, and others in the firm would be materially limited in pursuing the matter because of loyalty to that attorney, the personal disqualification of the attorney would be imputed to all others in the firm.

[4] The rule in section (a) of this Rule also does not prohibit representation by others in the law firm where the individual prohibited from involvement in a matter is a non-attorney, such as a paralegal or legal secretary. Nor does section (a) of this Rule prohibit representation if the attorney is prohibited from acting because of events before the individual became an attorney, for example, work that the individual did while a law student. Such individuals, however, ordinarily must be screened from any personal participation in the matter to avoid communication to others in the firm of confidential information that both the non- attorneys and the firm have a legal duty to protect. See Rules 19–301.0 (n) (1.0) and 19–305.3 (5.3).

[5] Rule 19–301.10 (b) (1.10) operates to permit a law firm, under certain circumstances, to represent a person with interests directly adverse to those of a client represented by an attorney who formerly was associated with the firm. The Rule applies regardless of when the formerly associated attorney represented the client. However, the law firm may not represent a person with interests adverse to those of a present client of the firm, which would violate Rule 19–301.7 (1.7). Moreover, the firm may not represent the person where the matter is the same or substantially related to that in which the formerly associated attorney represented the client and any other attorney currently in the firm has material information protected by Rules 19–301.6 (1.6) and 19–301.9 (c) (1.9).

[6] Where the conditions of section (c) of this Rule are met, imputation is removed, and consent to the new representation is not required. Attorneys should be aware, however, that courts may impose more stringent obligations in ruling upon motions to disqualify an attorney from pending litigation.

[7] Requirements for screening procedures are stated in Rule 19–301.0 (n) (1.0). Section (c) of this Rule does not prohibit the screened

attorney from receiving a salary or partnership share established by prior independent agreement, but that attorney may not receive compensation directly related to the matter in which the attorney is disqualified.

[8] Rule 19–301.10 (d) (1.10) removes imputation with the informed consent of the affected client or former client under the conditions stated in Rule 19–301.7 (1.7). The conditions stated in Rule 19–301.7 (1.7) require the attorney to determine that the representation is not prohibited by Rule 19–301.7 (b) (1.7) and that each affected client or former client has given informed consent to the representation, confirmed in writing. In some cases, the risk may be so severe that the conflict may not be cured by client consent. For a discussion of the effectiveness of client waivers of conflicts that might arise in the future, see Rule 19–301.7 (1.7), Comment [22]. For a definition of informed consent, see Rule 19–301.0 (g) (1.0).

[9] Where an attorney has joined a private firm after having represented the government, imputation is governed by Rule 19–301.11 (b) and (c) (1.11), not this Rule. Under Rule 19–301.11 (d) (1.11), where an attorney represents the government after having served clients in private practice, nongovernmental employment, or in another government agency, former-client conflicts are not imputed to government attorneys associated with the individually disqualified attorney.

[10] Where an attorney is prohibited from engaging in certain transactions under Rule 19–301.8 (1.8), section (j) of that Rule, and not this Rule, determines whether that prohibition also applies to other attorneys associated in a firm with the personally prohibited attorney.

♦ ♦ ♦

Model Rules Comparison: Rule 19–301.10 (1.10) is substantially similar to the language of the Ethics 2000 Amendments to the ABA Model Rules of Professional Conduct except for changes to Comment [1] and to provide for screening in Rule 19–301.10 (c) (1.10) and Comments [6] and [7], with the appropriate redesignation of sections. These screening provisions, along with Rule 19–301.0 (n) (1.0) and Comments [9]-[11] under Rule 19–301.0 (1.0) are substantially the same as former Rule 1.10

(b) (adopted January 1, 2000) with additional guidance on how to make screening effective.

RULE 1.11

Special Conflicts of Interest for Former and Current Government Officers and Employees

(a) Except as law may otherwise expressly permit, an attorney who has formerly served as a public officer or employee of the government:

(1) is subject to Rule 19–301.9 (c) (1.9); and

(2) shall not otherwise represent a client in connection with a matter in which the attorney participated personally and substantially as a public officer or employee, unless the appropriate government agency gives its informed consent, confirmed in writing, to the representation.

(b) When an attorney is disqualified from representation under section (a) of this Rule, no attorney in a firm with which that attorney is associated may knowingly undertake or continue representation in such a matter unless:

(1) the disqualified attorney is timely screened from any participation in the matter and is apportioned no part of the fee therefrom; and

(2) written notice is promptly given to the appropriate government agency to enable it to ascertain compliance with this Rule.

(c) Except as law may otherwise expressly permit, an attorney having information that the attorney knows is confidential government information about a person acquired when the attorney was a public officer or employee, may not represent a private client whose interests are adverse to that person in a matter in which the information could be used to the material disadvantage of that person. As used in this Rule, the term "confidential government information" means information that has been obtained under governmental authority and which, at the time this Rule is applied, the government is prohibited by law from disclosing to the public or has a legal privilege not to disclose and which is not otherwise available to the public. A firm with which that attorney is associated may undertake or continue representation in the matter only if the disqualified attorney is timely screened from any participation in the matter and is apportioned no part of the fee therefrom.

(d) Except as law may otherwise expressly permit, an attorney currently serving as a public officer or employee:

(1) is subject to Rules 19–301.7 (1.7) and 19–301.9 (1.9); and

(2) shall not:

(A) participate in a matter in which the attorney participated personally and substantially while in private practice or non- governmental employment, unless the appropriate government agency gives its informed consent, confirmed in writing; or

(B) negotiate for private employment with any person who is involved as a party or as an attorney for a party in a matter in which the attorney is participating personally and substantially, except that an attorney serving as a law clerk to a judge, other adjudicative officer or arbitrator may negotiate for private employment as permitted by Rule 19–301.12 (b) (1.12) and subject to the conditions stated in Rule 19–301.12 (b) (1.12).

(e) As used in this Rule, the term "matter" includes:

(1) any judicial or other proceeding, application, request for a ruling or other determination, contract, claim, controversy, investigation, charge, accusation, arrest or other particular matter involving a specific party or parties, and

(2) any other matter covered by the conflict of interest rules of the appropriate government agency.

COMMENT

[1] An attorney who has served or is currently serving as a public officer or employee is personally subject to the Maryland Attorneys' Rules of Professional Conduct, including the prohibition against concurrent conflicts of interest stated in Rule 19–301.7 (1.7). In addition, such an attorney may be subject to statutes and

government regulations regarding conflict of interest. Such statutes and regulations may circumscribe the extent to which the government agency may give consent under this Rule. See Rule 19–301.0 (g) (1.0) for the definition of informed consent.

[2] Subsections (a)(1), (a)(2) and (d)(1) of this Rule restate the obligations of an individual attorney who has served or is currently serving as an officer or employee of the government toward a former government or private client. Rule 19–301.10 (1.10) is not applicable to the conflicts of interest addressed by this Rule. Rather, section (b) of this Rule sets forth a special imputation rule for former government attorneys that provides for screening and notice. Because of the special problems raised by imputation within a government agency, section (d) of this Rule does not impute the conflicts of an attorney currently serving as an officer or employee of the government to other associated government officers or employees, although ordinarily it will be prudent to screen such attorneys.

[3] Subsections (a)(2) and (d)(2) of this Rule apply regardless of whether an attorney is adverse to a former client and are thus designed not only to protect the former client, but also to prevent an attorney from exploiting public office for the advantage of another client. For example, an attorney who has pursued a claim on behalf of the government may not pursue the same claim on behalf of a later private client after the attorney has left government service, except when authorized to do so by the government agency under section (a) of this Rule. Similarly, an attorney who has pursued a claim on behalf of a private client may not pursue the claim on behalf of the government, except when authorized to do so by section (d). As with subsections (a)(1) and (d)(1) of this Rule, Rule 19–301.10 (1.10) is not applicable to the conflicts of interest addressed by these subsections.

[4] This Rule represents a balancing of interests. On the one hand, where the successive clients are a government agency and another client, public or private, the risk exists that power or discretion vested in that agency might be used for the special benefit of the other client. An attorney should not be in a position where benefit to the other client might affect performance of the attorney's

professional functions on behalf of the government. Also, unfair advantage could accrue to the other client by reason of access to confidential government information about the client's adversary obtainable only through the attorney's government service. On the other hand, the rules governing attorneys presently or formerly employed by a government agency should not be so restrictive as to inhibit transfer of employment to and from the government. The government has a legitimate need to attract qualified attorneys as well as to maintain high ethical standards. Thus a former government attorney is disqualified only from particular matters in which the attorney participated personally and substantially. The provisions for screening and waiver in section (b) of this Rule are necessary to prevent the disqualification rule from imposing too severe a deterrent against entering public service. The limitation of disqualification in subsections (a)(2) and (d)(2) of this Rule to matters involving a specific party or parties, rather than extending disqualification to all substantive issues on which the attorney worked, serves a similar function.

[5] When an attorney has been employed by one government agency and then moves to a second government agency, it may be appropriate to treat that second agency as another client for purposes of this Rule, as when an attorney is employed by a city and subsequently is employed by a federal agency. However, because the conflict of interest is governed by section (d) of this Rule, the latter agency is not required to screen the attorney as section (b) of this Rule requires a law firm to do. The question of whether two government agencies should be regarded as the same or different clients for conflict of interest purposes is beyond the scope of these Rules. See Rule 19–301.13 (1.13) Comment [8].

[6] Sections (b) and (c) of this Rule contemplate a screening arrangement. See Rule 19–301.0 (n) (1.0) (requirements for screening procedures). These sections do not prohibit an attorney from receiving a salary or partnership share established by prior independent agreement, but that attorney may not receive compensation directly relating the attorney's compensation to the fee in the matter in which the attorney is disqualified.

[7] Notice, including a description of the screened attorney's prior representation and of the screening procedures employed, generally should be given as soon as practicable after the need for screening becomes apparent.

[8] Section (c) of this Rule operates only when the attorney in question has knowledge of the information, which means actual knowledge; it does not operate with respect to information that merely could be imputed to the attorney.

[9] Sections (a) and (d) of this Rule do not prohibit an attorney from jointly representing a private party and a government agency when doing so is permitted by Rule 19–301.7 (1.7) and is not otherwise prohibited by law.

[10] For purposes of section (e) of this Rule, a "matter" may continue in another form. In determining whether two particular matters are the same, the attorney should consider the extent to which the matters involve the same basic facts, the same or related parties, and the time elapsed.

♦ ♦ ♦

Model Rules Comparison: Rule 19–301.11 (1.11) is substantially similar to the language of the Ethics 2000 Amendments to the ABA Model Rules of Professional Conduct.

RULE 1.12

Former Judge, Arbitrator, Mediator or Other Third-Party Neutral

(a) Except as stated in section (d) of this Rule, an attorney shall not represent anyone in connection with a matter in which the attorney participated personally and substantially as a judge or other adjudicative officer or law clerk to such a person or as an arbitrator, mediator or other third-party neutral, unless all parties to the proceeding give informed consent, confirmed in writing.

(b) An attorney shall not negotiate for employment with any person who is involved as a party or as an attorney for a party in a matter in which the attorney is participating personally and substantially as a judge or other adjudicative officer or as an arbitrator, mediator or other third-party neutral. An attorney serving as a law clerk to a judge or other adjudicative officer may negotiate for employment with a party or attorney involved in a matter in which the clerk is participating personally and substantially, but only after the attorney has notified the judge or other adjudicative officer.

(c) If an attorney is disqualified by section (a) of this Rule, no attorney in a firm with which that attorney is associated may knowingly undertake or continue representation in the matter unless:

(1) the disqualified attorney is timely screened from any participation in the matter and is apportioned no part of the fee therefrom; and

(2) written notice is promptly given to the parties and any appropriate tribunal to enable them to ascertain compliance with this Rule.

(d) An arbitrator selected as a partisan of a party in a multimember arbitration panel is not prohibited from subsequently representing that party.

COMMENT

[1] This Rule generally parallels Rule 19–301.11 (1.11). The term "personally and substantially" signifies that a judge who was a member of a multimember court, and thereafter left judicial office to practice law, is not prohibited from representing a client in a matter pending in the court, but in which the former judge did not participate. So also the fact that a former judge exercised administrative responsibility in a court does not prevent the former judge from acting as an attorney in a matter where the judge had previously exercised remote or incidental administrative responsibility that did not affect the merits. Compare the Comment to Rule 19–301.11 (1.11).

[2] The term "adjudicative officer" includes such officials as judges pro tempore, referees, special magistrates, hearing officers, and other parajudicial officers, and also attorneys who serve as part-time judges. See Title 18, Chapter 200, Maryland Code of Conduct for Judicial Appointees.

[3] Like former judges, attorneys who have served as arbitrators, mediators, or other third-party neutrals may be asked to represent a client in a matter in which the attorney participated personally and substantially. This Rule forbids such representation unless all of the parties to the proceedings give their informed consent, confirmed in writing. See Rule 19–301.0 (g) and (b) (1.0). Other law or codes of ethics governing third-party neutrals may impose more stringent standards of personal or imputed disqualification. See Rule 19–302.4 (2.4).

[4] Although attorneys who serve as third-party neutrals do not have information concerning the parties that is protected under Rule 19–301.6 (1.6), they typically owe the parties an obligation of confidentiality under law or codes of ethics governing third- party neutrals. Thus, section (c) of this Rule provides that conflicts of the personally disqualified attorney will be imputed to other attorneys in a law firm unless the conditions of this section are met.

[5] Requirements for screening procedures are stated in Rule 19–301.0 (n) (1.0). Subsection (c)(1) of this Rule does not prohibit the screened attorney from receiving a salary or partnership share established by prior independent agreement, but that attorney may not receive compensation directly related to the matter in which the attorney is disqualified.

[6] Notice, including a description of the screened attorney's prior representation and of the screening procedures employed, generally should be given as soon as practicable after the need for screening becomes apparent.

♦ ♦ ♦

Model Rules Comparison: Apart from redesignating the sections of the Comments to this Rule, Rule 19–301.12 (1.12) is substantially similar to the language of the Ethics 2000 Amendments to the ABA Model Rules of Professional Conduct.

RULE 1.13

ORGANIZATION AS CLIENT

(a) An attorney employed or retained by an organization represents the organization acting through its duly authorized constituents.

(b) If an attorney for an organization knows that an officer, employee or other person associated with the organization is engaged in action, intends to act or refuses to act in a matter related to the representation that is a violation of a legal obligation to the organization, or a violation of law that reasonably might be imputed to the organization, and is likely to result in substantial injury to the organization, the attorney shall proceed as is reasonably necessary in the best interest of the organization. Unless the attorney reasonably believes that it is not necessary in the best interest of the organization to do so, the attorney shall refer the matter to higher authority in the organization, including, if warranted by the circumstances, to the highest authority that can act on behalf of the organization as determined by applicable law.

(c) When the organization's highest authority insists upon action, or refuses to take action, that is clearly a violation of a legal obligation to the organization, or a violation of law which reasonably might be imputed to the organization, and is reasonably certain to result in substantial injury to the organization, the attorney may take further remedial action that the attorney reasonably believes to be in the best interest of the organization. Such action may include revealing information otherwise protected by Rule 19–301.6 (1.6) only if the attorney reasonably believes that:

(1) the highest authority in the organization has acted to further the personal or financial interests of members of the authority which are in conflict with the interests of the organization; and

(2) revealing the information is necessary in the best interest of the organization.

(d) In dealing with an organization's directors, officers, employees, members, shareholders or other constituents, an attorney shall explain the identity of the client when the attorney knows or reasonably should know that the organization's interests are adverse to those of the constituents with whom the attorney is dealing.

(e) An attorney representing an organization may also represent any of its directors, officers, employees, members, shareholders or other constituents, subject to the provisions of Rule 19–301.7 (1.7). If the organization's consent to the dual representation is required by Rule

19–301.7 (1.7), the consent shall be given by an appropriate official of the organization other than the individual who is to be represented, or by the shareholders.

COMMENT

The Entity as the Client

[1] An organizational client is a legal entity, but it cannot act except through its officers, directors, employees, shareholders and other constituents.

[2] Officers, directors, employees and shareholders are the constituents of the corporate organizational client. The duties created by this Rule apply equally to unincorporated associations. "Other constituents" as used in this Comment means the positions equivalent to officers, directors, employees and shareholders held by persons acting for organizational clients that are not corporations.

[3] When one of the constituents of an organizational client communicates with the organization's attorney in that person's organizational capacity, the communication is protected by Rule 19–301.6 (1.6). Thus, for example, if an organizational client requests its attorney to investigate allegations of wrongdoing, interviews made in the course of that investigation between the attorney and the client's employees or other constituents are covered by Rule 19–301.6 (1.6). This does not mean, however, that constituents of an organizational client are the clients of the attorney. The attorney may not disclose to such constituents information relating to the representation except for disclosures explicitly or impliedly authorized by the organizational client in order to carry out the representation or as otherwise permitted by Rule 19–301.6 (1.6).

[4] When constituents of the organization make decisions for it, the decisions ordinarily must be accepted by the attorney even if their utility or prudence is doubtful. Decisions concerning policy and operations, including ones entailing serious risk, are not as such in the attorney's province. However, different considerations arise

when the attorney knows that the organization is likely to be substantially injured by action of a constituent that is in violation of law. In such a circumstance, it may be reasonably necessary for the attorney to ask the constituent to reconsider the matter. If that fails, or if the matter is of sufficient seriousness and importance to the organization, it may be reasonably necessary for the attorney to take steps to have the matter reviewed by a higher authority in the organization, depending on the seriousness of the matter and whether the constituent in question has apparent motives to act at variance with the organization's interest. Review by the chief executive officer or by the board of directors may be required when the matter is of importance commensurate with their authority. At some point it may be useful or essential to obtain an independent legal opinion.

[5] The organization's highest authority to whom a matter may be referred ordinarily will be the board of directors or similar governing body. However, applicable law may prescribe that under certain conditions the highest authority reposes elsewhere; for example, in the independent directors of a corporation.

[6] If an attorney can take remedial action without a disclosure of information that might adversely affect the organization, the attorney as a matter of professional discretion may take such action as the attorney reasonably believes to be in the best interest of the organization. For example, an attorney for a close corporation may find it reasonably necessary to disclose misconduct by the Board to the shareholders. However, taking such action could entail disclosure of information relating to the representation with consequent risk of injury to the client; when such is the case, the organization is threatened by alternative injuries; the injury that may result from the governing Board's action or refusal to act, and the injury that may result if the attorney's remedial efforts entail disclosure of confidential information. The attorney may pursue remedial efforts even at the risk of disclosure in the circumstances stated in subsections (c)(1) and (c)(2) of this Rule.

Relation to Other Rules

[7] The authority and responsibility provided in this Rule are concurrent with the authority and responsibility provided in other Rules. Section (c) of this Rule supplements Rule 19–301.6 (b) (1.6) by providing an additional basis upon which the attorney may reveal information relating to the representation, but does not modify, restrict, or limit the provisions of Rule 19–301.6 (b)(1)-(6) (1.6). Under section (c) of this Rule the attorney may reveal such information only when the organization's highest authority insists upon or fails to address threatened or ongoing action that is clearly a violation of law, and then only to the extent the attorney reasonably believes necessary to prevent reasonably certain substantial injury to the organization. It is not necessary that the attorney's services be used in furtherance of the violation as it is under Rules 19–301.6 (b)(2) (1.6) and 19–301.6 (b)(3) (1.6), but it is required that the matter be related to the attorney's representation of the organization. In particular, this Rule does not limit or expand the attorney's responsibility under Rules 19–301.8 (1.8), 19–301.16 (1.16), 19–303.3 (3.3) or 19–304.1 (4.1). If the attorney's services are being used by an organization to further a crime or fraud by the organization, Rules 19–301.6 (b)(2) (1.6) and 19–301.6 (b)(3) (1.6) may permit the attorney to disclose information otherwise protected by Rule 19–301.6 (a) (1.6). In such circumstances, Rule 19–301.2 (d) (1.2) may also be applicable.

Government Agency

[8] The duty defined in this Rule applies to governmental organizations. Defining precisely the identity of the client and prescribing the resulting obligations of such attorneys may be more difficult in the government context and is a matter beyond the scope of these Rules. See Scope [18]. Although in some circumstances the client may be a specific agency, it may also be a branch of government, such as the executive branch, or the government as a whole. For example, if the action or failure to act involves the head of a bureau, either the department of which

the bureau is a part or the relevant branch of government may be the client for purposes of this Rule. Moreover, in a matter involving the conduct of government officials, a government attorney may have authority under applicable law to question such conduct more extensively than that of an attorney for a private organization in similar circumstances. Thus, when the client is a governmental organization, a different balance may be appropriate between maintaining confidentiality and assuring that the wrongful act is prevented or rectified, for public business is involved. In addition, duties of attorneys employed by the government or attorneys in military service may be defined by statutes and regulation. This Rule does not limit that authority. See Scope.

Clarifying the Attorney's Role

[9] There are times when the organization's interest may be or become adverse to those of one or more of its constituents. In such circumstances the attorney should advise any constituent, whose interest the attorney finds adverse to that of the organization of the conflict or potential conflict of interest, that the attorney cannot represent such constituent, and that such person may wish to obtain independent representation. Care must be taken to assure that the individual understands that, when there is such adversity of interest, the attorney for the organization cannot provide legal representation for that constituent individual, and that discussions between the attorney for the organization and the individual may not be privileged.

[10] Whether such a warning should be given by the attorney for the organization to any constituent individual may turn on the facts of each case.

Dual Representation

[11] Section (e) of this Rule recognizes that an attorney for an organization may also represent a principal officer or major shareholder.

Derivative Actions

[12] Under generally prevailing law, the shareholders or members of a corporation may bring suit to compel the directors to perform their legal obligations in the supervision of the organization. Members of unincorporated associations have essentially the same right. Such an action may be brought nominally by the organization, but usually is, in fact, a legal controversy over management of the organization.

[13] The question can arise whether an attorney for the organization may defend such an action. The proposition that the organization is the attorney's client does not alone resolve the issue. Most derivative actions are a normal incident of an organization's affairs, to be defended by the organization's attorney like any other suit. However, if the claim involves serious charges of wrongdoing by those in control of the organization, a conflict may arise between the attorney's duty to the organization and the attorney's relationship with the board. In those circumstances, Rule 19–301.7 (1.7) governs who may represent the directors and the organization.

♦ ♦ ♦

Model Rules Comparison: Rule 19–301.13 (1.13) retains elements of existing Maryland language, incorporates further revisions, and incorporates language in Rule 1.13 (d) and Comments [5] and [8] from the Ethics 2000 Amendments to the ABA Model Rules.

RULE 1.14

Client with Diminished Capacity

(a) When a client has diminished capacity, the attorney shall, as far as reasonably possible, maintain a typical client-attorney relationship with the client.

(b) When the attorney reasonably believes that the client has diminished capacity, is at risk of substantial physical, financial, or other harm unless action is taken, and cannot adequately act in the client's own interest, the attorney may take reasonably necessary protective action to address those risks.

(c) Information relating to the representation of a client with diminished capacity is protected by Rule 19–301.6 (1.6). When taking protective action pursuant to section (b) of this Rule, the attorney is impliedly authorized under Rule 19–301.6 (a) (1.6) to reveal information about the client, but only to the extent reasonably necessary to protect the client's interests.

COMMENT

[1] The typical client-attorney relationship is based on the assumption that the client, when properly advised and assisted, is capable of making decisions about important matters. See Rule 19–300.1. When the client has diminished capacity, however, maintaining the typical client-attorney relationship may not be possible in all respects. In particular, a severely incapacitated individual may have limited or no ability to make legally binding decisions. Nevertheless, to an increasing extent the law recognizes intermediate degrees of capacity. Indeed, a client with diminished capacity often has the ability to understand, deliberate upon, and reach conclusions about matters affecting the client's own well-being. A client with diminished capacity also may have such ability with supported decision-making or other accommodations. For example, it is recognized that some individuals can be quite capable of handling routine financial matters while needing special legal protection concerning more complex transactions. In addition, children as young as five or six years of age, and certainly those of ten or twelve, are regarded as having opinions that are entitled to weight in legal proceedings concerning their custody or their property. Consideration of and, when appropriate, deference to these opinions are especially important in cases involving children in Child In Need of Assistance (CINA) and related Termination of Parental Rights (TPR) and adoption proceedings. With respect to these categories of cases, the Maryland Foster Care Court Improvement Project has prepared Guidelines of Advocacy for Attorneys Representing Children in CINA and Related TPR and Adoption Proceedings. The Guidelines are included in an appendix to the Maryland Rules. Also included in an Appendix to the Maryland Rules are

Maryland Guidelines for Practice for Court-Appointed Attorneys Representing Children in Cases Involving Child Custody or Child Access, developed by the Maryland Judicial Conference Committee on Family Law. When representing a minor or alleged disabled person in a guardianship proceeding, the attorney should be familiar with and follow the Maryland Guidelines for Attorneys Representing Minors and Alleged Disabled Persons in Guardianship Proceedings, an appendix to Title 10 of the Maryland Rules.

[2] The fact that a client suffers a disability does not diminish the attorney's obligation to treat the client with attention and respect. Even if the individual has a legal representative, the attorney should as far as possible accord the represented individual the status of client, particularly in maintaining communication.

[3] The client may wish to have family members or other individuals participate in discussions with the attorney. When necessary to assist in the representation, the presence of such individuals generally does not affect the applicability of the attorney-client evidentiary privilege. Nevertheless, the attorney must keep the client's interests foremost and, except for protective action authorized under section (b) of this Rule, must look to the client, and not family members, to make decisions on the client's behalf.

[4] If a legal representative has already been appointed for the client, the attorney should ordinarily look to the representative for decisions on behalf of the client. In matters involving a minor, whether the attorney should look to the parents as natural guardians may depend on the type of proceeding or matter in which the attorney is representing the minor. If the attorney represents the guardian as distinct from the ward, and is aware that the guardian is acting adversely to the ward's interest, the attorney may have an obligation to prevent or rectify the guardian's misconduct. See Rule 19–301.2 (d) (1.2).

Taking Protective Action

[5] If an attorney reasonably believes that a client is at risk of substantial physical, financial or other harm unless action is taken, and that a normal client-attorney relationship cannot be maintained as

provided in section (a) of this Rule because the client lacks sufficient capacity to communicate or to make adequately considered decisions in connection with the representation, then section (b) of this Rule permits the attorney to take protective measures deemed necessary. Such measures could include: consulting with family members, delaying action if feasible to permit clarification or improvement of circumstances, using voluntary surrogate decision-making tools such as durable powers of attorney or consulting with support groups, professional services, adult-protective agencies or other individuals or entities that have the ability to protect the client. In taking any protective action, the attorney should be guided by such factors as the wishes and values of the client to the extent known, the client's best interests and the goals of intruding into the client's decision-making autonomy to the least extent feasible, maximizing client capacities and respecting the client's family and social connections.

[6] In determining the extent of the client's diminished capacity, the attorney should consider and balance such factors as: the client's ability to articulate reasoning leading to a decision; variability of state of mind and ability to appreciate consequences of a decision; the substantive fairness of a decision; and the consistency of a decision with the known long-term commitments and values of the client. In appropriate circumstances, the attorney may seek guidance from an appropriate diagnostician.

[7] If a legal representative has not been appointed, the attorney should consider whether appointment of a guardian ad litem, conservator or guardian is necessary to protect the client's interests. Thus, if a client with diminished capacity has substantial property that should be sold for the client's benefit, effective completion of the transaction may require appointment of a legal representative. In addition, rules of procedure in litigation sometimes provide that minors or individuals with diminished capacity must be represented by a guardian or next friend if they do not have a general guardian. In many circumstances, however, appointment of a legal representative may be more expensive or traumatic for the client than circumstances in fact require. Evaluation of such circumstances is a

matter entrusted to the professional judgment of the attorney. In considering alternatives, however, the attorney should be aware of any law that requires the attorney to advocate the least restrictive action on behalf of the client.

Disclosure of the Client's Condition

[8] Disclosure of the client's diminished capacity could adversely affect the client's interests. For example, raising the question of diminished capacity could, in some circumstances, lead to proceedings for involuntary commitment. Information relating to the representation is protected by Rule 19–301.6 (1.6). Therefore, unless authorized to do so, the attorney may not disclose such information. When taking protective action pursuant to section (b) of this Rule, the attorney is impliedly authorized to make the necessary disclosures, even when the client directs the attorney to the contrary. Nevertheless, given the risks of disclosure, section (c) of this Rule limits what the attorney may disclose in consulting with other individuals or entities or seeking the appointment of a legal representative. At the very least, the attorney should determine whether it is likely that the person or entity consulted with will act adversely to the client's interests before discussing matters related to the client. The attorney's position in such cases is an unavoidably difficult one.

Emergency Legal Assistance

[9] In an emergency where the health, safety or a financial interest of an individual with seriously diminished capacity is threatened with imminent and irreparable harm, an attorney may take legal action on behalf of such an individual even though the individual is unable to establish a client-attorney relationship or to make or express considered judgments about the matter, when the individual or another acting in good faith on that individual's behalf has consulted with the attorney. Even in such an emergency, however, the attorney should not act unless the attorney reasonably believes that the individual has no other attorney, agent, or other representative available. The attorney should take legal action on behalf of the

individual only to the extent reasonably necessary to maintain the status quo or otherwise avoid imminent and irreparable harm. An attorney who undertakes to represent a an individual in such an exigent situation has the same duties under these Rules as the attorney would with respect to a client.

[10] An attorney who acts on behalf of an individual with seriously diminished capacity in an emergency should keep the confidences of the individual as if dealing with a client, disclosing them only to the extent necessary to accomplish the intended protective action. The attorney should disclose to any tribunal involved and to any other attorney involved the nature of his or her relationship with the individual. The attorney should take steps to regularize the relationship or implement other protective solutions as soon as possible.

♦ ♦ ♦

Model Rules Comparison: Rule 19–301.14 (1.14) is substantially similar to the language of the Ethics 2000 Amendments to the ABA Model Rules of Professional Conduct, with the exception of retaining elements of existing Maryland language in Comment [1] and further revising Comments [5] and [10].

RULE 1.15

SAFEKEEPING PROPERTY

(a) An attorney shall hold property of clients or third persons that is in an attorney's possession in connection with a representation separate from the attorney's own property. Funds shall be kept in a separate account maintained pursuant to Title 19, Chapter 400 of the Maryland Rules, and records shall be created and maintained in accordance with the Rules in that Chapter. Other property shall be identified specifically as such and appropriately safeguarded, and records of its receipt and distribution shall be created and maintained. Complete records of the account funds and of other property shall be kept by the attorney and shall be preserved for a period of at least five years after the date the record was created.

(b) An attorney may deposit the attorney's own funds in a client trust account only as permitted by Rule 19–408 (b).

(c) Unless the client gives informed consent, confirmed in writing, to a different arrangement, an attorney shall deposit legal fees and expenses that have been paid in advance into a client trust account and may withdraw those funds for the attorney's own benefit only as fees are earned or expenses incurred.

(d) Upon receiving funds or other property in which a client or third person has an interest, an attorney shall promptly notify the client or third person. Except as stated in this Rule or otherwise permitted by law or by agreement with the client, an attorney shall deliver promptly to the client or third person any funds or other property that the client or third person is entitled to receive and, upon request by the client or third person, shall render promptly a full accounting regarding such property.

(e) When an attorney in the course of representing a client is in possession of property in which two or more persons (one of whom may be the attorney) claim interests, the property shall be kept separate by the attorney until the dispute is resolved. The attorney shall distribute promptly all portions of the property as to which the interests are not in dispute.

♦ ♦ ♦

Cross reference: For the duties of an attorney with respect to attorney trust account funds that are presumed abandoned, see Rule 19–414.

COMMENT

[1] An attorney should hold property of others with the care required of a professional fiduciary. Securities should be kept in a safe deposit box, except when some other form of safekeeping is warranted by special circumstances. All property of clients or third persons, including prospective clients, must be kept separate from the attorney's business and personal property and, if money, in one or more trust accounts. Separate trust accounts may be warranted when administering estate money or acting in similar fiduciary capacities. An attorney should maintain on a current basis books and records in accordance with generally accepted accounting practice and the Rules in Title 19, Chapter 400 and

comply with any other record-keeping rules established by law or court order.

[2] Normally it is impermissible to commingle the attorney's own funds with client funds, and section (b) of this Rule provides that it is permissible only as permitted by Rule 19–408 (b). Accurate records must be kept regarding which part of the funds are the attorney's.

[3] Section (c) of Rule 19–301.15 (1.15) permits advances against unearned fees and unincurred costs to be treated as either the property of the client or the property of the attorney. Unless the client gives informed consent, confirmed in writing, to a different arrangement, the Rule's default position is that such advances be treated as the property of the client, subject to the restrictions provided in section (a) of this Rule. In any case, at the termination of an engagement, advances against fees that have not been incurred must be returned to the client as provided in Rule 19–301.16 (d) (1.16).

[4] Attorneys often receive funds from which the attorney's fee will be paid. The attorney is not required to remit the client funds that the attorney reasonably believes represent fees owed. However, an attorney may not hold funds to coerce a client into accepting the attorney's contention. The disputed portion of the funds must be kept in a trust account and the attorney should suggest means for prompt resolution of the dispute, such as arbitration. The undisputed portion of the funds shall be distributed promptly.

[5] Section (e) of this Rule also recognizes that third parties may have lawful claims against specific funds or other property in a attorney's custody, such as a client's creditor who has a lien on funds recovered in a personal injury action. An attorney may have a duty under applicable law to protect such third-party claims against wrongful interference by the client. In such cases, when the third-party claim is not frivolous under applicable law, the attorney must refuse to surrender the funds or property to the client until the claims are resolved. An attorney should not unilaterally assume to arbitrate a dispute between the client and the third party, but, when there are substantial grounds for dispute as to the person entitled

to the funds, the attorney may file an action to have a court resolve the dispute.

[6] The obligations of an attorney under this Rule are independent of those arising from activity other than rendering legal services. For example, an attorney who serves only as an escrow agent is governed by the applicable law relating to fiduciaries even though the attorney does not render legal services in the transaction and is not governed by this Rule.

♦ ♦ ♦

Model Rules Comparison: Rule 19–301.15 (1.15) is substantially similar to the language of the Ethics 2000 Amendments to the ABA Model Rules of Professional Conduct, with the exception of changes to Rule 19–301.15 (c) (1.15), the addition of Comment [3], and the omission of ABA Comment [6].

RULE 1.16

DECLINING OR TERMINATING REPRESENTATION

(a) Except as stated in section (c) of this Rule, an attorney shall not represent a client or, where representation has commenced, shall withdraw from the representation of a client if:

(1) the representation will result in violation of the Maryland Attorneys' Rules of Professional Conduct or other law;

(2) the attorney's physical or mental condition materially impairs the attorney's ability to represent the client; or

(3) the attorney is discharged.

(b) Except as stated in section (c) of this Rule, an attorney may withdraw from representing a client if:

(1) withdrawal can be accomplished without material adverse effect on the interests of the client;

(2) the client persists in a course of action involving the attorney's services that the attorney reasonably believes is criminal or fraudulent;

(3) the client has used the attorney's services to perpetrate a crime or fraud;

(4) the client insists upon action or inaction that the attorney considers repugnant or with which the attorney has a fundamental disagreement;

(5) the client fails substantially to fulfill an obligation to the attorney regarding the attorney's services and has been given reasonable warning that the attorney will withdraw unless the obligation is fulfilled;

(6) the representation will result in an unreasonable financial burden on the attorney or has been rendered unreasonably difficult by the client; or

(7) other good cause for withdrawal exists.

(c) An attorney must comply with applicable law requiring notice to or permission of a tribunal when terminating representation. When ordered to do so by a tribunal, an attorney shall continue representation notwithstanding good cause for terminating the representation.

(d) Upon termination of representation, an attorney shall take steps to the extent reasonably practicable to protect a client's interests, such as giving reasonable notice to the client, allowing time for employment of another attorney, surrendering papers and property to which the client is entitled and refunding any advance payment of fee or expense that has not been earned or incurred. The attorney may retain papers relating to the client to the extent permitted by other law.

COMMENT

[1] An attorney should not accept representation in a matter unless it can be performed competently, promptly, without improper conflict of interest and to completion. Ordinarily, a representation in a matter is completed when the agreed-upon assistance has been concluded. See Rules 19–301.2 (c) (1.2) and 19–306.5 (6.5). See also Rule 19–301.3 (1.3), Comment [4].

Mandatory Withdrawal

[2] An attorney ordinarily must decline or withdraw from representation if the client demands that the attorney engage in conduct

that is illegal or violates the Maryland Attorneys' Rules of Professional Conduct or other law. The attorney is not obligated to decline or withdraw simply because the client suggests such a course of conduct; a client may make such a suggestion in the hope that an attorney will not be constrained by a professional obligation.

[3] When an attorney has been appointed to represent a client, withdrawal ordinarily requires approval of the appointing authority. See also Rule 19–306.2 (6.2). Similarly, court approval or notice to the court is often required by applicable law before an attorney withdraws from pending litigation. Difficulty may be encountered if withdrawal is based on the client's demand that the attorney engage in unprofessional conduct. The court may request an explanation for the withdrawal, while the attorney may be bound to keep confidential the facts that would constitute such an explanation. The attorney's statement that professional considerations require termination of the representation ordinarily should be accepted as sufficient. Attorneys should be mindful of their obligation to both clients and the court under Rules 19–301.6 (1.6) and 19–303.3 (3.3).

Discharge

[4] A client has a right to discharge an attorney at any time, with or without cause, subject to liability for payment for the attorney's services. Where future dispute about the withdrawal may be anticipated, it may be advisable to prepare a written statement reciting the circumstances.

[5] Whether a client can discharge an appointed attorney may depend on applicable law. A client seeking to do so should be given a full explanation of the consequences. These consequences may include a decision by the appointing authority that appointment of successor attorney is unjustified, thus requiring self-representation by the client.

[6] If the client has severely diminished capacity, the client may lack the legal capacity to discharge the attorney, and in any event the

discharge may be seriously adverse to the client's interests. The attorney should make special effort to help the client consider the consequences and may take reasonably necessary protective action as provided in Rule 19–301.14 (1.14).

Optional Withdrawal

[7] An attorney may withdraw from representation in some circumstances. The attorney has the option to withdraw if it can be accomplished without material adverse effect on the client's interests. Withdrawal is also justified if the client persists in a course of action that the attorney reasonably believes is criminal or fraudulent, for a an attorney is not required to be associated with such conduct even if the attorney does not further it. Withdrawal is also permitted if the attorney's services were misused in the past even if that would materially prejudice the client. The attorney may also withdraw where the client insists on taking action or inaction that the attorney considers repugnant or with which the attorney has a fundamental disagreement.

[8] An attorney may withdraw if the client refuses to abide by the terms of an agreement relating to the representation, such as an agreement concerning fees or court costs or an agreement limiting the objectives of the representation.

Assisting the Client Upon Withdrawal

[9] Even if the attorney has been unfairly discharged by the client, an attorney must take all reasonable steps to mitigate the consequences to the client. The attorney may retain papers as security for a fee only to the extent permitted by law, subject to the limitations in section (d) of this Rule. See Rule 19–301.15 (1.15).

♦ ♦ ♦

Model Rules Comparison: Rule 19–301.16 (1.16) is substantially similar to the language of the Ethics 2000 Amendments to the ABA Model Rules of Professional Conduct with the exception of the addition of "or inaction" to Rule 19–301.16 (b)(4) (1.16) and Comment [7], and the addition of "subject to the limitations in section (d) of this Rule" to Comment [9].

RULE 1.17

SALE OF LAW PRACTICE

(a) Subject to section (b) of this Rule, a law practice, including goodwill, may be sold if the following conditions are satisfied:

(1) Except in the case of death, disability, or appointment of the seller to judicial office, the entire practice that is the subject of the sale has been in existence at least five years prior to the date of sale;

(2) The practice is sold as an entirety to another attorney or law firm; and

(3) Written notice has been mailed to the last known address of the seller's current clients regarding:

(A) the proposed sale;

(B) the terms of any proposed change in the fee arrangement;

(C) the client's right to retain another attorney, to take possession of the file, and to obtain any funds or other property to which the client is entitled; and

(D) the fact that the client's consent to the new representation will be presumed if the client does not take any action or does not otherwise object within sixty (60) days of mailing of the notice.

(b) If a notice required by subsection (a)(3) of this Rule is returned and the client cannot be located, the representation of that client may be transferred to the purchaser only by an order of a court of competent jurisdiction authorizing the transfer. The seller may disclose to the court in camera information relating to the representation only to the extent necessary to obtain an order authorizing the transfer.

COMMENT

[1] The practice of law is a profession, not merely a business. Clients are not commodities that can be purchased and sold at will. Pursuant to this Rule, when an attorney or an entire firm ceases to practice and another attorney or firm takes over the representation,

the selling attorney or firm may obtain compensation for the reasonable value of the practice as may withdrawing partners of law firms. See Rules 19–305.4 (5.4) and 19–305.6 (5.6).

Termination of Practice by the Seller

[2] The requirement that all of the private practice be sold is satisfied if the seller in good faith makes the entire practice available for sale to the purchaser. The fact that a number of the seller's clients decide not to be represented by the purchaser but take their matters elsewhere does not therefore result in a violation. The purchase agreement for the sale of a law practice may allow for restrictions on the scope and time of the seller's reentry into practice.

Single Purchaser

[3] The Rule requires a single purchaser. The prohibition against piecemeal sale of a practice protects those clients whose matters are less lucrative and who might find it difficult to secure another attorney if a sale could be limited to substantial fee-generating matters. The purchaser is required to undertake all client matters in the practice, subject to client consent. If, however, the purchaser is unable to undertake all client matters because of a conflict of interest in a specific matter respecting which the purchaser is not permitted by Rule 19–301.7 (1.7) or another rule to represent the client, the requirement that there be a single purchaser is nevertheless satisfied.

Client Confidences, Consent and Notice

[4] Negotiations between seller and prospective purchaser prior to disclosure of information relating to a specific representation of an identifiable client no more violate the confidentiality provisions of Rule 19–301.6 (1.6) than do preliminary discussions concerning the possible association of another attorney or mergers between firms, with respect to which client consent is not required. Providing the purchaser access to client-specific information relating to the representation and to the file, however, requires client consent.

The Rule provides that before such information can be disclosed by the seller to the purchaser, written notice of the contemplated sale must be mailed to the client. The notice must include the identity of the purchaser and any proposed change in the terms of future representation, and must tell the client that the decision to consent or make other arrangements must be made within 60 days. If nothing is heard from the client within that time, consent to the new representation is presumed.

[5] An attorney or law firm ceasing to practice cannot be required to remain in practice because some clients cannot be given actual notice of the proposed purchase. Since these clients cannot themselves consent to the new representation or direct any other disposition of their files, the Rule requires an order from a court having jurisdiction authorizing their transfer or other disposition. The Court can be expected to determine whether reasonable efforts to locate the client have been exhausted, and whether the absent client's legitimate interests will be served by authorizing the transfer of the file so that the purchaser may continue the representation. Preservation of client confidences requires that the petition for a court order be considered in camera.

[6] All the elements of client autonomy, including the client's absolute right to discharge an attorney and transfer the representation to another, survive the sale of the practice. Additionally, the transfer of the practice does not operate to change the attorney-client privilege.

Other Applicable Ethical Standards

[7] Attorneys participating in the sale of a law practice are subject to the ethical standards applicable to the involvement of another attorney in the representation of a client. These include, for example, the seller's obligation to exercise competence in identifying a purchaser qualified to assume the practice and the purchaser's obligation to undertake the representation competently (see Rule 19–301.1 (1.1)); the obligation to avoid disqualifying

conflicts, and to secure the client's informed consent for those conflicts which can be agreed to (see Rule 19–301.7 (1.7) regarding conflicts and Rule 19–301.0 (g) (1.0) for the definition of informed consent); and the obligation to protect information relating to the representation (see Rules 19–301.6 (1.6) and 19–301.9 (1.9)).

[8] If approval of the substitution of the purchasing attorney for the selling attorney is required by the rules of any tribunal in which a matter is pending, that approval must be obtained before the matter can be included in the sale (see Rule 19–301.16 (1.16)).

Applicability of the Rule

[9] This Rule applies to the sale of a law practice by representatives of a deceased or disabled attorney, or one who has disappeared. Thus, the seller may be represented by a non-attorney representative not subject to these Rules. Since, however, no attorney may participate in a sale of a law practice that does not conform to the requirements of this Rule, the representatives of the seller as well as the purchasing attorney can be expected to see to it that the requirements are met.

[10] Admission to or retirement from law partnership or professional association, retirement plans and similar arrangements, and a sale of tangible assets of a law practice, do not constitute a sale or purchase governed by this Rule.

[11] This Rule does not apply to the transfers of legal representation between attorneys when such transfers are unrelated to the sale of a practice. This Rule does not prohibit an attorney from selling his or her interest in a law practice.

♦ ♦ ♦

Committee note: The sale of a practice does not mean that the appearance of an attorney who is in a case will be stricken.

Model Rules Comparison: This Rule substantially retains Maryland language as it existed prior to the Ethics 2000 Amendments to the ABA Model Rules of Professional Conduct except for incorporating ABA changes to Comments [2] and [3].

RULE 1.18

DUTIES TO PROSPECTIVE CLIENT

(a) A person who discusses with an attorney the possibility of forming a client-attorney relationship with respect to a matter is a prospective client.

(b) Even when no client-attorney relationship ensues, an attorney who has had discussions with a prospective client shall not use or reveal information learned in the consultation, except as Rule 19–301.9 (1.9) would permit with respect to information of a former client.

(c) An attorney subject to section (b) of this Rule shall not represent a client with interests materially adverse to those of a prospective client in the same or a substantially related matter if the attorney received information from the prospective client that could be significantly harmful to that person in the matter, except as provided in section (d) of this Rule. If an attorney is disqualified from representation under this section, no attorney in a firm with which that attorney is associated may knowingly undertake or continue representation in such a matter, except as provided in section (d) of this Rule.

(d) Representation is permissible if both the affected client and the prospective client have given informed consent, confirmed in writing, or the disqualified attorney is timely screened from any participation in the matter and is apportioned no part of the fee therefrom.

COMMENT

[1] Prospective clients, like clients, may disclose information to an attorney, place documents or other property in the attorney's custody, or rely on the attorney's advice. An attorney's discussions with a prospective client usually are limited in time and depth and leave both the prospective client and the attorney free (and sometimes required) to proceed no further. Hence, prospective clients should receive some but not all of the protection afforded clients.

[2] Not all persons who communicate information to an attorney are entitled to protection under this Rule. For example, a person who

communicates information unilaterally to an attorney, without any reasonable expectation that the attorney is willing to discuss the possibility of forming a client-attorney relationship, is not a "prospective client" within the meaning of section (a) of this Rule.

[3] It is often necessary for a prospective client to reveal information to the attorney during an initial consultation prior to the decision about formation of a client-attorney relationship. The attorney often must learn such information to determine whether there is a conflict of interest with an existing client and whether the matter is one that the attorney is willing to undertake. Section (b) of this Rule prohibits the attorney from using or revealing that information, except as permitted by Rule 19–301.9 (1.9), even if the client or attorney decides not to proceed with the representation. The duty exists regardless of how brief the initial conference may be.

[4] In order to avoid acquiring disqualifying information from a prospective client, an attorney considering whether or not to undertake a new matter should limit the initial interview to only such information as reasonably appears necessary for that purpose. Where the information indicates that a conflict of interest or other reason for non-representation exists, the attorney should so inform the prospective client or decline the representation. If the prospective client wishes to retain the attorney, and if consent is possible under Rule 19–301.7 (1.7), then consent from all affected present or former clients must be obtained before accepting the representation.

[5] An attorney may condition conversations with a prospective client on the person's informed consent that no information disclosed during the consultation will prohibit the attorney from representing a different client in the matter. See Rule 19–301.0(g) (1.0) for the definition of informed consent. If the agreement expressly so provides, the prospective client may also consent to the attorney's subsequent use of information received from the prospective client.

[6] Even in the absence of an agreement, under section (c) of this Rule, the attorney is not prohibited from representing a client with interests adverse to those of the prospective client in the same or a substantially related matter unless the attorney has received

from the prospective client information that could be significantly harmful if used in the matter.

[7] Under section (c) of this Rule, the prohibition in this Rule is imputed to other attorneys as provided in Rule 19–301.10 (1.10), but, under section (d) of this Rule, imputation may be avoided if the attorney obtains the informed consent, confirmed in writing, of both the prospective and affected clients. In the alternative, imputation may be avoided if, under section (d) of this Rule, all disqualified attorneys are timely screened. See Rule 19–301.0 (n) (1.0) (requirements for screening procedures). Section (d) of this Rule does not prohibit the screened attorney from receiving a salary or partnership share established by prior independent agreement, but that attorney may not receive compensation directly related to the matter in which the attorney is disqualified.

[8] For the duty of competence of an attorney who gives assistance on the merits of a matter to a prospective client, see Rule 19–301.1 (1.1). For an attorney's duties when a prospective client entrusts valuables or papers to the attorney's care, see Rule 19–301.15 (1.15).

♦ ♦ ♦

Model Rules Comparison: This Rule, newly added to the Model Rules by the Ethics 2000 Amendments to the ABA Model Rules of Professional Conduct, is substantially similar to the ABA Rule, with the exception of omitting portions of ABA Model Rule 1.18(d) and Comment [7], and omitting ABA Comment [8] with appropriate redesignation of the Comment section thereafter.

COUNSELOR

RULE 2.1

ADVISOR

In representing a client, an attorney shall exercise independent professional judgment and render candid advice. In rendering advice, an attorney may refer not only to law but to other considerations such as moral, economic, social and political factors, that may be relevant to the client's situation.

COMMENT

Scope of Advice

[1] A client is entitled to straightforward advice expressing the attorney's honest assessment. Legal advice often involves unpleasant facts and alternatives that a client may be disinclined to confront. In presenting advice, an attorney endeavors to sustain the client's morale and may put advice in as acceptable a form as honesty permits. However, an attorney should not be deterred from giving candid advice by the prospect that the advice will be unpalatable to the client.

[2] Advice couched in narrow legal terms may be of little value to a client, especially where practical considerations, such as cost or effects on other people, are predominant. Purely technical legal advice, therefore, can sometimes be inadequate. It is proper for an attorney to refer to relevant moral and ethical considerations in giving advice. Although an attorney is not a moral advisor as such, moral and ethical considerations impinge upon most legal questions and may decisively influence how the law will be applied.

[3] A client may expressly or impliedly ask the attorney for purely technical advice. When such a request is made by a client experienced in legal matters, the attorney may accept it at face value. When such a request is made by a client inexperienced in legal matters, however, the attorney's responsibility as advisor may include indicating that more may be involved than strictly legal considerations.

[4] Matters that go beyond strictly legal questions may also be in the domain of another profession. Family matters can involve problems within the professional competence of psychiatry, clinical psychology or social work; business matters can involve problems within the competence of the accounting profession or of financial specialists. Where consultation with a professional in another field is itself something a competent attorney would recommend, the attorney should make such a recommendation. At the same time,

an attorney's advice at its best often consists of recommending a course of action in the face of conflicting recommendations of experts.

Offering Advice

[5] In general, an attorney is not expected to give advice until asked by the client. However, when an attorney knows that a client proposes a course of action that is likely to result in substantial adverse legal consequences to the client, the attorney's duty to the client under Rule 19–301.4 (1.4) may require that the attorney offer advice if the client's course of action is related to the representation. Similarly, when a matter is likely to involve litigation and, in the opinion of the attorney, one or more forms of alternative dispute resolution are reasonable alternatives to litigation, the attorney should advise the client about those reasonable alternatives. An attorney ordinarily has no duty to initiate investigation of a client's affairs or to give advice that the client has indicated is unwanted, but an attorney may initiate advice to a client when doing so appears to be in the client's interest.

♦ ♦ ♦

Model Rules Comparison: Rule 19–302.1 (2.1) is substantially similar to the language of the Ethics 2000 Amendments to the ABA Model Rules of Professional Conduct.

RULE 2.2

[DELETED]

RULE 2.3

Evaluation for Use by Third Parties

(a) An attorney may provide an evaluation of a matter affecting a client for the use of someone other than the client if the attorney reasonably believes that making the evaluation is compatible with other aspects of the attorney's relationship with the client.

(b) When the attorney knows or reasonably should know that the evaluation is likely to affect the client's interests materially and adversely, the attorney shall not provide the evaluation unless the client gives informed consent.

(c) Except as disclosure is authorized in connection with a report of an evaluation, information relating to the evaluation is otherwise protected by Rule 19–301.6 (1.6).

COMMENT

Definition

[1] An evaluation may be performed at the client's direction or when impliedly authorized in order to carry out the representation. See Rule 19–301.2 (1.2). Such an evaluation may be for the primary purpose of establishing information for the benefit of third parties; for example, an opinion concerning the title of property rendered at the behest of a vendor for the information of a prospective purchaser, or at the behest of a borrower for the information of a prospective lender. In some situations, the evaluation may be required by a government agency; for example, an opinion concerning the legality of the securities registered for sale under the securities laws. In other instances, the evaluation may be required by a third person, such as a purchaser of a business.

[2] A legal evaluation should be distinguished from an investigation of a person with whom the attorney does not have a client- attorney relationship. For example, an attorney retained by a purchaser to analyze a vendor's title to property does not have a client-attorney relationship with the vendor. So also, an investigation into a person's affairs by a government attorney, or by special counsel employed by the government, is not an evaluation as that term is used in this Rule. The question is whether the attorney is retained by the person whose affairs are being examined. When the attorney is retained by that person, the general rules concerning loyalty to client and preservation of confidences apply, which is not the case if the attorney is retained by someone else. For this reason, it is essential to identify the person by whom the attorney is retained. This should be made clear not only to the person under examination, but also to others to whom the results are to be made available.

Duties Owed to Third Person and Client

[3] When the evaluation is intended for the information or use of a third person, a legal duty to that person may or may not arise. That legal question is beyond the scope of this Rule. However, since such an evaluation involves a departure from the normal client-attorney relationship, careful analysis of the situation is required. The attorney must be satisfied as a matter of professional judgment that making the evaluation is compatible with other functions undertaken in behalf of the client. For example, if the attorney is acting as advocate in defending the client against charges of fraud, it would normally be incompatible with that responsibility for the attorney to perform an evaluation for others concerning the same or a related transaction. Assuming no such impediment is apparent, however, the attorney should advise the client of the implications of the evaluation, particularly the attorney's responsibilities to third persons and the duty to disseminate the findings.

Access to and Disclosure of Information

[4] The quality of an evaluation depends on the freedom and extent of the investigation upon which it is based. Ordinarily an attorney should have whatever latitude of investigation seems necessary as a matter of professional judgment. Under some circumstances, however, the terms of the evaluation may be limited. For example, certain issues or sources may be categorically excluded, or the scope of search may be limited by time constraints or the noncooperation of persons having relevant information. Any such limitations which are material to the evaluation should be described in the report. If after an attorney has commenced an evaluation, the client refuses to comply with the terms upon which it was understood the evaluation was to have been made, the attorney's obligations are determined by law, having reference to the terms of the client's agreement and the surrounding circumstances. In no circumstances is the attorney permitted to knowingly make a false statement of material fact or law in providing an evaluation under this Rule. See Rule 19–304.1 (4.1).

Obtaining Client's Informed Consent

[5] Information relating to an evaluation is protected by Rule 19–301.6 (1.6). In many situations, providing an evaluation to a third party poses no significant risk to the client; thus the attorney may be impliedly authorized to disclose information to carry out the representation. See Rule 19–301.6 (a) (1.6). Where, however, it is reasonably likely that providing the evaluation will affect the client's interests materially and adversely, the attorney must first obtain the client's consent after the client has been adequately informed concerning the important possible effects on the client's interests. See Rules 19–301.6 (a) (1.6) and 19–301.0 (g) (1.0).

Financial Auditors' Requests for Information

[6] When a question concerning the legal situation of a client arises at the instance of the client's financial auditor and the question is referred to the attorney, the attorney's response may be made in accordance with procedures recognized in the legal profession. Such a procedure is set forth in the American Bar Association Statement of Policy Regarding Lawyers' Responses to Auditors' Requests for Information.

♦ ♦ ♦

Model Rules Comparison: Rule 19–302.3 (2.3) is substantially similar to the language of the Ethics 2000 Amendments to the ABA Model Rules of Professional Conduct.

RULE 2.4

Attorney Serving as Third-Party Neutral

(a) An attorney serves as a third-party neutral when the attorney assists two or more persons who are not clients of the attorney to reach a resolution of a dispute or other matter that has arisen between them. Service as a third-party neutral may include service as an arbitrator, a mediator or in such other capacity as will enable the attorney to assist the parties to resolve the matter.

(b) An attorney serving as a third-party neutral shall inform unrepresented parties that the attorney is not representing them. When the attorney knows or reasonably should know that a party does not understand the attorney's role in the matter, the attorney shall explain the difference between the attorney's role as a third-party neutral and an attorney's role as one who represents a client.

COMMENT

[1] Alternative dispute resolution has become a substantial part of the civil justice system. Aside from representing clients in dispute-resolution processes, attorneys often serve as third-party neutrals. A third-party neutral is an individual, such as a mediator, arbitrator, conciliator or evaluator, who assists the parties, represented or unrepresented, in the resolution of a dispute or in the arrangement of a transaction. Whether a third-party neutral serves primarily as a facilitator, evaluator or decision maker depends on the particular process that is either selected by the parties or mandated by a court.

[2] The role of a third-party neutral is not unique to attorneys, although, in some court-connected contexts, only attorneys are allowed to serve in this role or to handle certain types of cases. In performing this role, the attorney may be subject to court rules or other law that apply either to third-party neutrals generally or to attorneys serving as third-party neutrals. See Title 17 of the Md. Rules. Attorney-neutrals may also be subject to various codes of ethics, such as the Maryland Standards of Conduct for Mediators, Arbitrators and Other ADR Practitioners adopted by the Maryland Supreme Court or the Code of Ethics for Arbitration in Commercial Disputes prepared by a joint committee of the American Bar Association and the American Arbitration Association.

[3] Unlike non-attorneys who serve as third-party neutrals, attorneys serving in this role may experience unique problems as a result of differences between the role of a third-party neutral and an attorney's service as a client representative. The potential for confusion is significant when the parties are unrepresented in the process. Thus, section (b) of this Rule requires an attorney-neutral to inform unrepresented parties that the attorney is not representing them. For some parties, particularly parties who frequently use

dispute-resolution processes, this information will be sufficient. For others, particularly those who are using the process for the first time, more information may be required. Where appropriate, the attorney should inform unrepresented parties of the important differences between the attorney's role as third-party neutral and an attorney's role as a client representative, including the inapplicability of the attorney-client evidentiary privilege. The extent of disclosure required under this section will depend on the particular parties involved and the subject matter of the proceeding, as well as the particular features of the dispute-resolution process selected.

[4] An attorney who serves as a third-party neutral subsequently may be asked to serve as an attorney representing a client in the same matter. The conflicts of interest that arise for both the individual attorney and the attorney's law firm are addressed in Rule 19–301.12 (1.12).

[5] Attorneys who represent clients in alternative dispute-resolution processes are governed by the Maryland Attorneys' Rules of Professional Conduct. When the dispute-resolution process takes place before a tribunal, as in binding arbitration (see Rule 19–301.0 (p) (1.0)), the attorney's duty of candor is governed by Rule 19–303.3 (3.3). Otherwise, the attorney's duty of candor toward both the third-party neutral and other parties is governed by Rule 19–304.1 (4.1).

♦ ♦ ♦

Model Rules Comparison: This Rule, newly added to the Model Rules by the Ethics 2000 Amendments to the ABA Model Rules of Professional Conduct, is substantially similar to the ABA Rule, with the exception of changing "will" to "may" in the fifth sentence of Comment [3].

ADVOCATE

RULE 3.1

MERITORIOUS CLAIMS AND CONTENTIONS

An attorney shall not bring or defend a proceeding, or assert or controvert an issue therein, unless there is a basis for doing so that is not frivolous, which includes, for example, a good faith argument for an extension, modification or reversal of existing law. An attorney may nevertheless so defend the proceeding as to require that every element of the moving party's case be established.

COMMENT

[1] The advocate has a duty to use legal procedure for the fullest benefit of the client's cause, but also a duty not to abuse legal procedure. The law, both procedural and substantive, establishes the limits within which an advocate may proceed. However, the law is not always clear and never is static. Accordingly, in determining the proper scope of advocacy, account must be taken of the law's ambiguities and potential for change.

[2] The filing of an action or defense or similar action taken for a client is not frivolous merely because the facts have not first been fully substantiated or because the attorney expects to develop vital evidence only by discovery. What is required of attorneys, however, is that they inform themselves about the facts of their clients' cases and the applicable law and determine that they can make good faith arguments in support of their clients' positions. Such action is not frivolous even though the attorney believes that the client's position ultimately will not prevail. The action is frivolous, however, if the attorney is unable either to make a good faith argument on the merits of the action taken or to support the action taken by a good faith argument for an extension, modification or reversal of existing law.

[3] The attorney's obligations under this Rule are subordinate to federal or state constitutional law that entitles a defendant in a criminal matter to the assistance of an attorney in presenting a claim that otherwise would be prohibited by this Rule.

♦ ♦ ♦

Model Rules Comparison: This Rule substantially retains Maryland language as it existed prior to the Ethics 2000 Amendments to the ABA Model Rules of Professional Conduct except for: (1) adding "for example" to the text of the Rule; and (2) incorporating ABA changes to Comments [2] and [3].

RULE 3.2

EXPEDITING LITIGATION

An attorney shall make reasonable efforts to expedite litigation consistent with the interests of the client.

COMMENT

[1] Dilatory practices bring the administration of justice into disrepute. Although there will be occasions when an attorney may properly seek a postponement for personal reasons, it is not proper for an attorney to routinely fail to expedite litigation solely for the convenience of the advocates. Nor will a failure to expedite be reasonable if done for the purpose of frustrating an opposing party's attempt to obtain rightful redress or repose. It is not a justification that similar conduct is often tolerated by the bench and bar. The question is whether a competent attorney acting in good faith would regard the course of action as having some substantial purpose other than delay. Financial or other benefit from otherwise improper delay in litigation is not a legitimate interest of the client.

♦ ♦ ♦

Model Rules Comparison: Rule 19–303.2 (3.2) is substantially similar to the language of the Ethics 2000 Amendments to the ABA Model Rules of Professional Conduct.

RULE 3.3

CANDOR TOWARD THE TRIBUNAL

(a) An attorney shall not knowingly:

(1) make a false statement of fact or law to a tribunal or fail to correct a false statement of material fact or law previously made to the tribunal by the attorney;

(2) fail to disclose a material fact to a tribunal when disclosure is necessary to avoid assisting a criminal or fraudulent act by the client;

(3) fail to disclose to the tribunal legal authority in the controlling jurisdiction known to the attorney to be directly adverse to the

position of the client and not disclosed by an opposing attorney; or

(4) offer evidence that the attorney knows to be false. If an attorney has offered material evidence and comes to know of its falsity, the attorney shall take reasonable remedial measures.

(b) The duties stated in section (a) of this Rule continue to the conclusion of the proceeding, and apply even if compliance requires disclosure of information otherwise protected by Rule 19–301.6 (1.6).

(c) An attorney may refuse to offer evidence that the attorney reasonably believes is false.

(d) In an ex parte proceeding, an attorney shall inform the tribunal of all material facts known to the attorney which will enable the tribunal to make an informed decision, whether or not the facts are adverse.

(e) Notwithstanding sections (a) through (d) of this Rule, an attorney for an accused in a criminal case need not disclose that the accused intends to testify falsely or has testified falsely if the attorney reasonably believes that the disclosure would jeopardize any constitutional right of the accused.

COMMENT

[1] This Rule governs the conduct of an attorney who is representing a client in the proceedings of a tribunal. See Rule 19–301.0(p) (1.0) for the definition of "tribunal." It also applies when the attorney is representing a client in an ancillary proceeding conducted pursuant to the tribunal's adjudicative authority, such as a deposition. Thus, for example, subsection (a)(4) of this Rule requires an attorney to take reasonable remedial measures if the attorney comes to know that a client who is testifying in a deposition has offered evidence that is false.

[2] This Rule sets forth special duties of attorneys as officers of the court to avoid conduct that undermines the integrity of the adjudicative process. An attorney acting as an advocate in an adjudicative proceeding has an obligation to present the client's case with persuasive force. Performance of that duty while maintaining confidences of the client, however, is qualified by the advocate's

duty of candor to the tribunal. Consequently, although an attorney in an adversary proceeding is not required to present an impartial exposition of the law or to vouch for the evidence submitted in a cause, the attorney must not allow the tribunal to be misled by false statements of law or fact or evidence that the attorney knows to be false.

Representations by an Attorney

[3] An advocate is responsible for pleadings and other documents prepared for litigation, but is usually not required to have personal knowledge of matters asserted therein, for litigation documents ordinarily present assertions by the client, or by someone on the client's behalf, and not assertions by the attorney. Compare Rule 19–303.1 (3.1). However, an assertion purporting to be on the attorney's own knowledge, as in an affidavit by the attorney or in a statement in open court, may properly be made only when the attorney knows the assertion is true or believes it to be true on the basis of a reasonably diligent inquiry. There are circumstances where failure to make a disclosure is the equivalent of an affirmative misrepresentation. The obligation prescribed in Rule 19–301.2 (d) (1.2) not to counsel a client to commit or assist the client in committing a fraud applies in litigation. Regarding compliance with Rule 19–301.2 (d) (1.2), see the Comment to that Rule. See also the Comment to Rule 19–308.4 (b) (8.4).

Misleading Legal Argument

[4] Legal argument based on a knowingly false representation of law constitutes dishonesty toward the tribunal. An attorney is not required to make a disinterested exposition of the law, but must recognize the existence of pertinent legal authorities. Furthermore, as stated in subsection (a)(3) of this Rule, an advocate has a duty to disclose directly adverse authority in the controlling jurisdiction which has not been disclosed by the opposing party. The underlying concept is that legal argument is a discussion seeking to determine the legal premises properly applicable to the case.

False Evidence

[5] When evidence that an attorney knows to be false is provided by a person who is not the client, the attorney must refuse to offer it regardless of the client's wishes.

[6] When false evidence is offered by the client, however, a conflict may arise between the attorney's duty to keep the client's revelations confidential and the duty of candor to the court. Upon ascertaining that material evidence is false, the attorney should seek to persuade the client that the evidence should not be offered or, if it has been offered, that its false character should immediately be disclosed. If the persuasion is ineffective, the attorney must take reasonable remedial measures.

[7] Except in the defense of a criminal accused, the rule generally recognized is that, if necessary to rectify the situation, an advocate must disclose the existence of the client's deception to the court or to the other party. Such a disclosure can result in grave consequences to the client, including not only a sense of betrayal but also loss of the case and perhaps a prosecution for perjury. But the alternative is that the attorney cooperate in deceiving the court, thereby subverting the truth-finding process which the adversary system is designed to implement. See Rule 19–301.2 (d) (1.2). Furthermore, unless it is clearly understood that the attorney will act upon the duty to disclose the existence of false evidence, the client can simply reject the attorney's advice to reveal the false evidence and insist that the attorney keep silent. Thus the client could in effect coerce the attorney into being a party to fraud on the court.

Perjury by a Criminal Defendant

[8] Whether an advocate for a criminally accused has the same duty of disclosure has been intensely debated. While it is agreed that the attorney should seek to persuade the client to refrain from perjurious testimony, there has been dispute concerning the attorney's duty when that persuasion fails. If the confrontation with the client occurs before trial, the attorney ordinarily can withdraw. Withdrawal before trial may not be possible, however, either because trial is imminent, or because the confrontation with the client does

not take place until the trial itself, or because no other attorney is available.

[9] The most difficult situation, therefore, arises in a criminal case where the accused insists on testifying when the attorney knows that the testimony is perjurious. The attorney's effort to rectify the situation can increase the likelihood of the client's being convicted as well as opening the possibility of a prosecution for perjury. On the other hand, if the attorney does not exercise control over the proof, the attorney participates, although in a merely passive way, in deception of the court.

[10] Three resolutions of this dilemma have been proposed. One is to permit the accused to testify by a narrative without guidance through the attorney's questioning. This compromises both contending principles; it exempts the attorney from the duty to disclose false evidence but subjects the client to an implicit disclosure of information imparted to the attorney. Another suggested resolution, of relatively recent origin, is that the advocate be entirely excused from the duty to reveal perjury if the perjury is that of the client. This is a coherent solution but makes the advocate a knowing instrument of perjury.

[11] The other resolution of the dilemma is that the attorney must reveal the client's perjury if necessary to rectify the situation. A criminal accused has a right to the assistance of an advocate, a right to testify and a right of confidential communication with an attorney. However, an accused should not have a right to assistance of an attorney in committing perjury. Furthermore, an advocate has an obligation, not only in professional ethics but under the law as well, to avoid implication in the commission of perjury or other falsification of evidence. See Rule 19–301.2 (d) (1.2).

Remedial Measures

[12] If perjured testimony or false evidence has been offered, the advocate's proper course ordinarily is to remonstrate with the client confidentially. If that fails, the advocate should seek to withdraw if that will remedy the situation. If withdrawal will not remedy the situation or is impossible, the advocate should make disclosure

to the court. It is for the court then to determine what should be done—making a statement about the matter to the trier of fact, ordering a mistrial or perhaps nothing. If the false testimony was that of the client, the client may controvert the attorney's version of their communication when the attorney discloses the situation to the court. If there is an issue whether the client has committed perjury, the attorney cannot represent the client in resolution of the issue, and a mistrial may be unavoidable. An unscrupulous client might in this way attempt to produce a series of mistrials and thus escape prosecution. However, a second such encounter could be construed as a deliberate abuse of the right to an attorney and as such a waiver of the right to further representation.

Constitutional Requirements

[13] The general rule—that an advocate must disclose the existence of perjury with respect to a material fact, even that of a client—applies to defense attorneys in criminal cases, as well as in other instances. However, the definition of the attorney's ethical duty in such a situation may be qualified by constitutional provisions for due process and the right to an attorney in criminal cases. Section (e) of this Rule is intended to protect from discipline the attorney who does not make disclosures mandated by sections (a) through (d) of this Rule only when the attorney acts in the "reasonable belief" that disclosure would jeopardize a constitutional right of the client. For a definition of "reasonable belief," see Rule 19–301.0 (l) (1.0).

Duration of Obligation

[14] A practical time limit on the obligation to rectify the presentation of false evidence has to be established. The conclusion of the proceeding is a reasonably definite point for the termination of the obligation. After that point, however, the attorney may be permitted to take certain actions pursuant to Rule 19–301.6 (b)(3) (1.6).

Refusing to Offer Proof Believed to Be False

[15] Generally speaking, an attorney has authority to refuse to offer testimony or other proof that the attorney reasonably believes is

false. Offering such proof may reflect adversely on the attorney's ability to discriminate in the quality of evidence and thus impair the attorney's effectiveness as an advocate. In criminal cases, however, an attorney may, in some jurisdictions, be denied this authority by constitutional requirements governing the right to an attorney.

Ex Parte Proceedings

[16] Ordinarily, an advocate has the limited responsibility of presenting one side of the matters that a tribunal should consider in reaching a decision; the conflicting position is expected to be presented by the opposing party. However, in an ex parte proceeding, such as an application for a temporary restraining order, there is no balance of presentation by opposing advocates. The object of an ex parte proceeding is nevertheless to yield a substantially just result. The judge has an affirmative responsibility to accord the absent party just consideration. The attorney for the represented party has the correlative duty to make disclosures of material facts known to the attorney and that the attorney reasonably believes are necessary to an informed decision.

♦ ♦ ♦

Model Rules Comparison: Rule 19–303.3 (3.3) has been rewritten to retain elements of existing Maryland language and to incorporate some changes from the Ethics 2000 Amendments to the ABA Model Rules.

RULE 3.4

Fairness to Opposing Party and Counsel

An attorney shall not:

(a) unlawfully obstruct another party's access to evidence or unlawfully alter, destroy or conceal a document or other material having potential evidentiary value. An attorney shall not counsel or assist another person to do any such act;

(b) falsify evidence, counsel or assist a witness to testify falsely, or offer an inducement to a witness that is prohibited by law;

(c) knowingly disobey an obligation under the rules of a tribunal except for an open refusal based on an assertion that no valid obligation exists;

(d) in pretrial procedure, make a frivolous discovery request or fail to make reasonably diligent effort to comply with a legally proper discovery request by an opposing party;

(e) in trial, allude to any matter that the attorney does not reasonably believe is relevant or that will not be supported by admissible evidence, assert personal knowledge of facts in issue except when testifying as a witness, or state a personal opinion as to the justness of a cause, the credibility of a witness, the culpability of a civil litigant or the guilt or innocence of an accused; or

(f) request a person other than a client to refrain from voluntarily giving relevant information to another party unless:

  (1) the person is a relative or an employee or other agent of a client; and

  (2) the attorney reasonably believes that the person's interests will not be adversely affected by refraining from giving such information.

COMMENT

[1] The procedure of the adversary system contemplates that the evidence in a case is to be marshalled competitively by the contending parties. Fair competition in the adversary system is secured by prohibitions against destruction or concealment of evidence, improperly influencing witnesses, obstructive tactics in discovery procedure, and the like.

[2] Documents and other items of evidence are often essential to establish a claim or defense. Subject to evidentiary privileges, the right of an opposing party, including the government, to obtain evidence through discovery or subpoena is an important procedural right. The exercise of that right can be frustrated if relevant material is altered, concealed or destroyed. Applicable law in many jurisdictions makes it an offense to destroy material for purpose of impairing its availability in a pending proceeding or one whose

commencement can be foreseen. Falsifying evidence is also generally a criminal offense. Section (a) of this Rule applies to evidentiary material generally, including computerized information.

[3] With regard to section (b) of this Rule, it is not improper to pay a witness's expenses, including lost earnings, or to compensate an expert witness on terms permitted by law. The common law rule in most jurisdictions is that it is improper to pay an occurrence witness any fee for testifying and that it is improper to pay an expert witness a contingent fee.

[4] Section (f) of this Rule permits an attorney to advise employees of a client to refrain from giving information to another party, for the employees may identify their interests with those of the client. See also Rule 19–304.2 (4.2).

♦ ♦ ♦

Model Rules Comparison: Rule 19–303.4 (3.4) is substantially similar to the language of the Ethics 2000 Amendments to the ABA Model Rules of Professional Conduct except that "including lost earnings" has been added to Comment [3] and the last two sentences of Comment [2] have been deleted.

RULE 3.5

IMPARTIALITY AND DECORUM OF THE TRIBUNAL

(a) An attorney shall not:

(1) seek to influence a judge, prospective, qualified, or sworn juror, or other official by means prohibited by law;

(2) before the trial of a case with which the attorney is connected, communicate outside the course of official proceedings with anyone known to the attorney to be on the jury list for trial of the case;

(3) during the trial of a case with which the attorney is connected, communicate outside the course of official proceedings with any member of the jury;

(4) during the trial of a case with which the attorney is not connected, communicate outside the course of official proceedings with any member of the jury about the case;

(5) after discharge of a jury from further consideration of a case with which the attorney is connected, ask questions of or make comments to a jury member that are calculated to harass or embarrass the jury member or to influence the jury member's actions in future jury service;

(6) conduct a vexatious or harassing investigation of any prospective, qualified, or sworn juror;

(7) communicate ex parte about an adversary proceeding with the judge or other official before whom the proceeding is pending, except as permitted by law;

(8) discuss with a judge potential employment of the judge if the attorney or a firm with which the attorney is associated has a matter that is pending before the judge; or

(9) engage in conduct intended to disrupt a tribunal.

(b) An attorney who has knowledge of any violation of section (a) of this Rule, any improper conduct by a prospective, qualified, or sworn juror or any improper conduct by another towards a prospective, qualified, or sworn juror, shall report it promptly to the court or other appropriate authority.

COMMENT

[1] Many forms of improper influence upon a tribunal are proscribed by criminal law. Others are specified in Title 18, Chapter 100, Maryland Code of Judicial Conduct, with which an advocate should be familiar. An attorney is required to avoid contributing to a violation of such provisions.

[2] The advocate's function is to present evidence and argument so that the cause may be decided according to law. Refraining from abusive or obstreperous conduct is a corollary of the advocate's right to speak on behalf of litigants. An attorney may stand firm against abuse by a judge but should avoid reciprocation; the judge's default is no justification for similar dereliction by an advocate. An advocate can present the cause, protect the record for subsequent review and preserve professional integrity

by patient firmness no less effectively than by belligerence or theatrics.

[3] With regard to the prohibition in subsection (a)(2) of this Rule against communications with anyone on "the jury list," see Md. Rules 2–512 (c) and 4–312 (c).

♦ ♦ ♦

Model Rules Comparison: Rule 19–303.5 (3.5) retains the former Maryland Rule text and comments, except that subsection (a)(8) is new and the reference in Comment [1] is to the Code of Judicial Conduct. Changes in ABA Model Rule 3.5 were not adopted.

RULE 3.6

TRIAL PUBLICITY

(a) An attorney who is participating or has participated in the investigation or litigation of a matter shall not make an extrajudicial statement that the attorney knows or reasonably should know will be disseminated by means of public communication and will have a substantial likelihood of materially prejudicing an adjudicative proceeding in the matter.

(b) Notwithstanding section (a) of this Rule, an attorney may state:

(1) the claim, offense or defense involved and, except when prohibited by law, the identity of the persons involved;

(2) information contained in a public record;

(3) that an investigation of a matter is in progress;

(4) the scheduling or result of any step in litigation;

(5) a request for assistance in obtaining evidence and information necessary thereto;

(6) a warning of danger concerning the behavior of a person involved, when there is reason to believe that there exists the likelihood of substantial harm to an individual or to the public interest; and

(7) in a criminal case, in addition to subsections (b)(1) through (6) of this Rule:

(A) the identity, residence, occupation and family status of the accused;

(B) if the accused has not been apprehended, information necessary to aid in apprehension of that person;

(C) the fact, time and place of arrest; and

(D) the identity of investigating and arresting officers or agencies and the length of the investigation.

(c) Notwithstanding section (a) of this Rule, an attorney may make a statement that a reasonable attorney would believe is required to protect a client from the substantial undue prejudicial effect of recent publicity not initiated by the attorney or the attorney's client. A statement made pursuant to this section shall be limited to such information as is necessary to mitigate the recent adverse publicity.

(d) No attorney associated in a firm or government agency with an attorney subject to section (a) of this Rule shall make a statement prohibited by section (a) of this Rule.

COMMENT

[1] It is difficult to strike a balance between protecting the right to a fair trial and safeguarding the right of free expression. Preserving the right to a fair trial necessarily entails some curtailment of the information that may be disseminated about a party prior to trial, particularly where trial by jury is involved. If there were no such limits, the result would be the practical nullification of the protective effect of the rules of forensic decorum and the exclusionary rules of evidence. On the other hand, there are vital social interests served by the free dissemination of information about events having legal consequences and about legal proceedings themselves. The public has a right to know about threats to its safety and measures aimed at assuring its security. It also has a legitimate interest in the conduct of judicial proceedings, particularly in matters of general public concern. Furthermore, the subject matter of legal proceedings is often of direct significance in debate and deliberation over questions of public policy.

[2] Special rules of confidentiality may validly govern proceedings in juvenile, domestic relations and mental disability proceedings, and perhaps other types of litigation. Rule 19–303.4 (c) (3.4) requires compliance with such rules.

[3] The Rule sets forth a basic general prohibition against an attorney's making statements that the attorney knows or should know will have a substantial likelihood of materially prejudicing an adjudicative proceeding. Recognizing that the public value of informed commentary is great and the likelihood of prejudice to a proceeding by the commentary of an attorney who is not involved in the proceeding is small, the rule applies only to attorneys who are, or who have been involved in the investigation or litigation of a case, and their associates.

[4] Section (b) of this Rule identifies specific matters about which an attorney's statements would not ordinarily be considered to present a substantial likelihood of material prejudice, and should not in any event be considered prohibited by the general prohibition of section (a) of this Rule. Section (b) of this Rule is not intended to be an exhaustive listing of the subjects upon which an attorney may make a statement, but statements on other matters may be subject to section (a) of this Rule.

[5] There are, on the other hand, certain subjects that are more likely than not to have a material prejudicial effect on a proceeding, particularly when they refer to a civil matter triable to a jury, a criminal matter, or any other proceeding that could result in incarceration. These subjects relate to:

(1) the character, credibility, reputation or criminal record of a party, suspect in a criminal investigation or witness, or the identity of a witness, or the expected testimony of a party or witness;

(2) in a criminal case or proceeding that could result in incarceration, the possibility of a plea of guilty to the offense or the existence or contents of any confession, admission, or statement given by a defendant or suspect or that person's refusal or failure to make a statement;

(3) the performance or results of any examination or test or the refusal or failure of a person to submit to an examination or test, or the identity or nature of physical evidence expected to be presented;

(4) any opinion as to the guilt or innocence of a defendant or suspect in a criminal case or proceeding that could result in incarceration;

(5) information that the attorney knows or reasonably should know is likely to be inadmissible as evidence in a trial and that would, if disclosed, create a substantial risk of prejudicing an impartial trial; or

(6) the fact that a defendant has been charged with a crime, unless there is included therein a statement explaining that the charge is merely an accusation and that the defendant is presumed innocent until and unless proven guilty.

[6] Another relevant factor in determining prejudice is the nature of the proceeding involved. Criminal jury trials will be most sensitive to extrajudicial speech. Civil trials may be less sensitive. Non-jury hearings and arbitration proceedings may be even less affected. The Rule will still place limitations on prejudicial comments in these cases, but the likelihood of prejudice may be different depending on the type of proceeding.

[7] Finally, extrajudicial statements that might otherwise raise a question under this Rule may be permissible when they are made in response to statements made publicly by another party, another party's attorney, or third persons, where a reasonable attorney would believe a public response is required in order to avoid prejudice to the attorney's client. When prejudicial statements have been publicly made by others, responsive statements may have the salutary effect of lessening any resulting adverse impact on the adjudicative proceeding. Such responsive statements should be limited to contain only such information as is necessary to mitigate undue prejudice created by the statements made by others.

[8] See Rule 19–303.8 (e) (3.8) for additional duties of prosecutors in connection with extrajudicial statements about criminal proceedings.

♦ ♦ ♦

Model Rules Comparison: Rule 19–303.6 (3.6) is substantially similar to the language of the Ethics 2000 Amendments to the ABA Model Rules of Professional Conduct.

RULE 3.7

ATTORNEY AS WITNESS

(a) An attorney shall not act as advocate at a trial in which the attorney is likely to be a necessary witness unless:

(1) the testimony relates to an uncontested issue;

(2) the testimony relates to the nature and value of legal services rendered in the case; or

(3) disqualification of the attorney would work substantial hardship on the client.

(b) An attorney may act as advocate in a trial in which another attorney in the attorney's firm is likely to be called as a witness unless precluded from doing so by Rule 19–301.7 (1.7) or Rule 19–301.9 (1.9).

COMMENT

[1] Combining the roles of advocate and witness can prejudice the tribunal and the opposing party and can also involve a conflict of interest between the attorney and client.

Advocate Witness Rule

[2] The tribunal has proper objection when the trier of fact may be confused or misled by a an attorney serving as both advocate and witness. The opposing party has proper objection where the combination of roles may prejudice that party's rights in the litigation. A witness is required to testify on the basis of personal knowledge, while an advocate is expected to explain and comment on evidence given by others. It may not be clear whether a statement by an

advocate-witness should be taken as proof or as an analysis of the proof.

[3] To protect the tribunal, section (a) of this Rule prohibits an attorney from simultaneously serving as advocate and necessary witness except in those circumstances specified in subsections (a)(1) through (a)(3) of this Rule. Subsection (a)(1) of this Rule recognizes that if the testimony will be uncontested, the ambiguities in the dual role are purely theoretical. Subsection (a)(2) of this Rule recognizes that where the testimony concerns the extent and value of legal services rendered in the action in which the testimony is offered, permitting the attorneys to testify avoids the need for a second trial with a new attorney to resolve that issue. Moreover, in such a situation the judge has firsthand knowledge of the matter in issue; hence, there is less dependence on the adversary process to test the credibility of the testimony.

[4] Apart from these two exceptions, subsection (a)(3) of this Rule recognizes that a balancing is required between the interests of the client and those of the tribunal and the opposing party. Whether the tribunal is likely to be misled or the opposing party is likely to suffer prejudice depends on the nature of the case, the importance and probable tenor of the attorney's testimony, and the probability that the attorney's testimony will conflict with that of other witnesses. Even if there is risk of such prejudice, in determining whether the attorney should be disqualified due regard must be given to the effect of disqualification on the attorney's client. It is relevant that one or both parties could reasonably foresee that the attorney would probably be a witness. The conflict of interest principles stated in prior, similar Rules 19–301.7 (1.7), 19–301.9 (1.9) and 19–301.10 (1.10) have no application to this aspect of the problem.

[5] Because the tribunal is not likely to be misled when an attorney acts as advocate in a trial in which another attorney in the attorney's firm will testify as a necessary witness, section (b) of this Rule permits the attorney to do so except in situations involving a conflict of interest.

Conflict of Interest

[6] In determining if it is permissible to act as advocate in a trial in which the attorney will be a necessary witness, the attorney must also consider that the dual role may give rise to a conflict of interest that will require compliance with Rules 19–301.7 (1.7) or 19–301.9 (1.9). For example, if there is likely to be substantial conflict between the testimony of the client and that of the attorney, the representation involves a conflict of interest that requires compliance with Rule 19–301.7 (1.7). This would be true even though the attorney might not be prohibited by section (a) of this Rule from simultaneously serving as advocate and witness because the attorney's disqualification would work a substantial hardship on the client. Similarly, an attorney who might be permitted to simultaneously serve as an advocate and a witness by subsection (a)(3) of this Rule might be precluded from doing so by Rule 19–301.9 (1.9). The problem can arise whether the attorney is called as a witness on behalf of the client or is called by the opposing party. Determining whether or not such a conflict exists is primarily the responsibility of the attorney involved. If there is a conflict of interest, the attorney must secure the client's informed consent, confirmed in writing. In some cases, the attorney will be precluded from seeking the client's consent. See Rule 19–301.7 (1.7). See Rule 19–301.0 (g) (1.0) for the definition of "confirmed in writing" and Rule 19–301.0 (f) (1.0) for the definition of "informed consent."

[7] Section (b) of this Rule provides that an attorney is not disqualified from serving as an advocate because an attorney with whom the attorney is associated in a firm is precluded from doing so by section (a) of this Rule. If, however, the testifying attorney would also be disqualified by Rule 19–301.7 (1.7) or Rule 19–301.9 (1.9) from representing the client in the matter, other attorneys in the firm will be precluded from representing the client by Rule 19–301.10 (1.10) unless the client gives informed consent under the conditions stated in Rule 19–301.7 (1.7).

♦ ♦ ♦

Model Rules Comparison: Rule 19–303.7 (3.7) is substantially similar to the language of the Ethics 2000 Amendments to the ABA Model Rules of Professional Conduct.

RULE 3.8

SPECIAL RESPONSIBILITIES OF A PROSECUTOR

The prosecutor in a criminal case shall:

(a) refrain from prosecuting a charge that the prosecutor knows is not supported by probable cause;

(b) make reasonable efforts to assure that the accused has been advised of the right to, and the procedure for obtaining, an attorney and has been given reasonable opportunity to obtain an attorney;

(c) not seek to obtain from an unrepresented accused a waiver of important pretrial rights, such as the right to a preliminary hearing;

(d) make timely disclosure to the defense of all evidence or information known to the prosecutor that tends to negate the guilt of the accused or mitigates the offense, and, in connection with sentencing, disclose to the defense and to the tribunal all unprivileged mitigating information known to the prosecutor, except when the prosecutor is relieved of this responsibility by a protective order of the tribunal;

(e) except for statements that are necessary to inform the public of the nature and extent of the prosecutor's action and that serve a legitimate law enforcement purpose, refrain from making extrajudicial comments that have a substantial likelihood of heightening public condemnation of the accused and exercise reasonable care to prevent an employee or other person under the control of the prosecutor in a criminal case from making an extrajudicial statement that the prosecutor would be prohibited from making under Rule 19–303.6 (3.6) or this Rule;

(f) when a prosecutor knows of new, credible, and material evidence creating a reasonable likelihood that a convicted defendant did not commit an offense of which the defendant was convicted, the prosecutor shall:

  (1) promptly disclose that evidence to an appropriate court or authority; and

(2) if the conviction was obtained in the prosecutor's jurisdiction:

(3) promptly disclose that evidence to the defendant unless a court authorizes delay; and

(4) undertake further investigation, or make reasonable efforts to cause an investigation, to determine whether the defendant was convicted of an offense that the defendant did not commit; and

(g) when a prosecutor knows of clear and convincing evidence establishing that a defendant in the prosecutor's jurisdiction was convicted of an offense that the defendant did not commit, the prosecutor shall seek to remedy the conviction.

COMMENT

[1] A prosecutor has the responsibility of a minister of justice and not simply that of an advocate. This responsibility carries with it specific obligations to see that the defendant is accorded procedural justice and that guilt is decided upon the basis of sufficient evidence. Precisely how far the prosecutor is required to go in this direction is a matter of debate and varies in different jurisdictions. Many jurisdictions have adopted the ABA Standards of Criminal Justice Relating to Prosecution Function, which in turn are the product of prolonged and careful deliberation by attorneys experienced in both criminal prosecution and defense. See also Rule 19–303.3 (d) (3.3), governing ex parte proceedings, among which grand jury proceedings are included. Applicable law may require other measures by the prosecutor and knowing disregard of those obligations or a systematic abuse of prosecutorial discretion could constitute a violation of Rule 19–308.4 (8.4).

[2] Section (c) of this Rule does not apply to an accused appearing self-represented with the approval of the tribunal. Nor does it forbid the lawful questioning of a suspect who has knowingly waived the rights to an attorney and silence.

[3] The exception in section (d) of this Rule recognizes that a prosecutor may seek an appropriate protective order from the tribunal if

disclosure of information to the defense could result in substantial harm to an individual or to the public interest.

[4] Section (e) of this Rule supplements Rule 19–303.6 (3.6), which prohibits extrajudicial statements that have a substantial likelihood of prejudicing an adjudicatory proceeding. In the context of a criminal prosecution, a prosecutor's extrajudicial statement can create the additional problem of increasing public condemnation of the accused. Although the announcement of an indictment, for example, will necessarily have severe consequences for the accused, a prosecutor can, and should, avoid comments which have no legitimate law enforcement purpose and have a substantial likelihood of increasing public opprobrium of the accused. Nothing in this Comment is intended to restrict the statements which a prosecutor may make which comply with Rule 19–303.6 (b) (3.6) or 19–303.6 (c) (3.6).

[5] Like other attorneys, prosecutors are subject to Rules 19–305.1 (5.1) and 19–305.3 (5.3), which relate to responsibilities regarding attorneys and non-attorneys who work for or are associated with the attorney's office. Section (e) of this Rule reminds the prosecutor of the importance of these obligations in connection with the unique dangers of improper extrajudicial statements in a criminal case. In addition, section (e) of this Rule requires a prosecutor to exercise reasonable care to prevent persons assisting or associated with the prosecutor from making improper extrajudicial statements, even when such persons are not under the direct supervision of the prosecutor. Ordinarily, the reasonable care standard will be satisfied if the prosecutor issues the appropriate cautions to law-enforcement personnel and other relevant individuals.

[6] When a prosecutor knows of new, credible, and material evidence creating a reasonable likelihood that a person outside the prosecutor's jurisdiction was convicted of a crime that the person did not commit, section (f) of this Rule requires prompt disclosure to the court or other appropriate authority, such as the chief prosecutor of the jurisdiction where the conviction occurred. If the conviction was obtained in the prosecutor's jurisdiction, section (f) of this Rule requires the prosecutor to examine the evidence and

undertake further investigation to determine whether the defendant is in fact innocent or make reasonable efforts to cause another appropriate authority to undertake the necessary investigation, and to promptly disclose the evidence to the court and, absent court-authorized delay, to the defendant. Consistent with the objectives of Rules 19–304.2 (4.2) and 19–304.3 (4.3), disclosure to a represented defendant must be made through the defendant's attorney, and, in the case of an unrepresented defendant, would ordinarily be accompanied by a request to a court for the appointment of an attorney to assist the defendant in taking such legal measures as may be appropriate.

[7] Under section (g) of this Rule, once the prosecutor knows of clear and convincing evidence that the defendant was convicted of an offense that the defendant did not commit, the prosecutor must seek to remedy the conviction. Necessary steps may include disclosure of the evidence to the defendant, requesting that the court appoint an attorney for an unrepresented indigent defendant and, where appropriate, notifying the court that the prosecutor has knowledge that the defendant did not commit the offense of which the defendant was convicted.

[8] A prosecutor's independent judgment, made in good faith, that the new evidence is not of such nature as to trigger the obligations of sections (f) and (g) of this Rule, though subsequently determined to have been erroneous, does not constitute a violation of this Rule.

♦ ♦ ♦

Model Rules Comparison: Rule 19–303.8 (3.8) has been rewritten to retain elements of existing Maryland language and to incorporate some changes from the Ethics 2000 Amendments to the ABA Model Rules and from the 2008 amendments to ABA Model Rule 3.8. ABA Model Rule 3.8 (e) has not been adopted.

RULE 3.9

ADVOCATE IN NONADJUDICATIVE PROCEEDINGS

An attorney representing a client before a legislative body or administrative agency in a nonadjudicative proceeding shall disclose that the appearance is in a representative capacity and shall conform to the provisions of Rules 19–303.3 (a) through(c) (3.3), 19–303.4 (a) through (c) (3.4), and 19–303.5 (3.5).

COMMENT

[1] In representation before bodies such as legislatures, municipal councils, and executive and administrative agencies acting in a rule-making or policy-making capacity, attorneys engage in activities that are comparable to those of an advocate appearing before a tribunal. For example, attorneys present facts, formulate issues and advance argument in the matters under consideration. The decision-making body, like a court, should be able to rely on the integrity of the submissions made to it. A An attorney appearing before such a body should deal with it honestly and in conformity with applicable rules of procedure.

[2] Given these policies, this Rule requires that an attorney who appears before legislative bodies or administrative agencies in such nonadjudicative proceedings must adhere to Rules 19–303.3 (a) through (c) (3.3), 19–303.4 (a) through (c) (3.4), and 19–303.5 (3.5). Attorneys appearing under these circumstances must also adhere to all other applicable Rules, including Rules 19–304.1 (4.1) through 19–304.4 (4.4).

[3] Attorneys have no exclusive right to appear before nonadjudicative bodies, as they do before a court. The requirements of this Rule therefore may subject attorneys to regulations inapplicable to advocates who are not attorneys.

[4] Not all appearances before a legislative body or administrative agency are nonadjudicative within the meaning of this Rule. This Rule only applies when an attorney represents a client in connection with an official or formal hearing or meeting to which the attorney or the attorney's client is presenting evidence or argument. Thus, this Rule does not apply to representation of a client in a negotiation or other bilateral transaction with a governmental agency; or in connection with an application for a license or other privilege or the client's compliance with generally applicable reporting requirements, such as the filing of income-tax returns. Nor does it apply to

the representation of a client in connection with an investigation or examination of the client's affairs conducted by government investigators or examiners. Representation in such matters is governed by Rules 19–304.1 (4.1) through 19–304.4 (4.4).

[5] When an attorney appears before a legislative body or administrative agency acting in an adjudicative capacity, the legislative body or administrative agency is considered a "Tribunal" for purposes of these Rules, and all Rules relating to representation by an attorney before a Tribunal apply. See Rule 19–301.0 (p) (1.0) for the definition of "Tribunal."

♦ ♦ ♦

Model Rules Comparison: Rule 19–303.9 (3.9) has been rewritten to retain elements of existing Maryland language, to incorporate some changes from the Ethics 2000 Amendments to the ABA Model Rules, and to incorporate further revisions.

TRANSACTIONS WITH PERSONS OTHER THAN CLIENTS

RULE 4.1

TRUTHFULNESS IN STATEMENTS TO OTHERS

(a) In the course of representing a client an attorney shall not knowingly:

(1) make a false statement of material fact or law to a third person; or

(2) fail to disclose a material fact when disclosure is necessary to avoid assisting a criminal or fraudulent act by a client.

(b) The duties stated in this Rule apply even if compliance requires disclosure of information otherwise protected by Rule 19–301.6 (1.6).

COMMENT

Misrepresentation

[1] An attorney is required to be truthful when dealing with others on a client's behalf, but generally has no affirmative duty to inform an opposing party of relevant facts. A misrepresentation can occur if the attorney incorporates or affirms a statement of another person

that the attorney knows is false. Misrepresentations can also occur by partially true but misleading statements or omissions that are the equivalent of affirmative false statements. For dishonest conduct that does not amount to a false statement or for misrepresentations by an attorney other than in the course of representing a client, see Rule 19–308.4 (8.4).

Statements of Fact

[2] This Rule refers to statements of fact. Whether a particular statement should be regarded as one of fact can depend on the circumstances. Under generally accepted conventions in negotiation, certain types of statements ordinarily are not taken as statements of material fact. Estimates of price or value placed on the subject of a transaction and a party's intentions as to an acceptable settlement of a claim are ordinarily in this category, and so is the existence of an undisclosed principal except where nondisclosure of the principal would constitute fraud. Attorneys should be mindful of their obligations under applicable law to avoid criminal or tortious misrepresentation.

Fraud by Client

[3] Under Rule 19–301.2 (d) (1.2), an attorney is prohibited from counseling or assisting a client in conduct that the attorney knows is criminal or fraudulent. Subsection (a)(2) of this Rule states a specific application of the principle set forth in Rule 19–301.2 (d) (1.2) and addresses the situation where a client's crime or fraud takes the form of a lie or misrepresentation. Sometimes an attorney can avoid assisting a client's crime or fraud by withdrawing from the representation. It also may be necessary for the attorney to give notice of the fact of withdrawal and to disaffirm an opinion, document, affirmation or the like. In extreme cases, however, substantive law may require an attorney to disclose information relating to the representation to avoid being deemed to have assisted the client's crime or fraud. If the attorney can avoid assisting a client's crime or fraud only by disclosing this information, then under section (b) of this Rule the attorney is required to do

so, even though the disclosure otherwise would be prohibited by Rule 19–301.6 (1.6).

Disclosure

[4] As noted in the comment to Rule 19–301.6 (1.6), the duty imposed by Rule 19–304.1 (4.1) may require an attorney to disclose information that otherwise is confidential and to correct or withdraw a statement. However, the constitutional rights of defendants in criminal cases may limit the extent to which an attorney for a defendant may correct a misrepresentation that is based on information provided by the client. See Comment to Rule 19–303.3 (3.3).

♦ ♦ ♦

Model Rules Comparison: Rule 19–304.1 (4.1) has been rewritten to retain elements of existing Maryland language, to incorporate some changes from the Ethics 2000 Amendments to the ABA Model Rules, and to incorporate further revisions.

RULE 4.2

Communication with Person Represented by Counsel

(a) Except as provided in section (c) of this Rule, in representing a client, an attorney shall not communicate about the subject of the representation with a person who the attorney knows is represented in the matter by another attorney unless the attorney has the consent of the other attorney or is authorized by law or court order to do so.

(b) If the person represented by another attorney is an organization, the prohibition extends to each of the organization's current officers, directors, and managing agents and (2) current agents or employees who supervise, direct, or regularly communicate with the organization's attorneys concerning the matter or whose acts or omissions in the matter may bind the organization for civil or criminal liability. The attorney may not communicate with a current agent or employee of the organization unless the attorney first has made inquiry to ensure that the agent or employee is not an individual with whom communication is prohibited by this section and has disclosed to the individual the attorney's identity and the fact that the attorney represents a client who has an interest adverse to the organization.

(c) An attorney may communicate with a government official about matters that are the subject of the representation if the government official has the authority to redress the grievances of the attorney's client and the attorney first makes the disclosures specified in section (b) of this Rule.

♦ ♦ ♦

Committee note: The use of the word "person" for "party" in section (a) of this Rule is not intended to enlarge or restrict the extent of permissible law enforcement activities of government attorneys under applicable judicial precedent.

COMMENT

[1] This Rule contributes to the proper functioning of the legal system by protecting a person who has chosen to be represented by an attorney in a matter against possible overreaching by other attorneys who are participating in the matter, interference by those attorneys with the attorney-client relationship, and the uncounseled disclosure of information relating to the representation.

[2] This Rule does not prohibit communication with a person, or an employee or agent of the person, concerning matters outside the representation. For example, the existence of a controversy between two organizations does not prohibit an attorney for either from communicating with non-attorney representatives of the other regarding a separate matter. Also, parties to a matter may communicate directly with each other and an attorney having independent justification or legal authorization for communicating with a represented person is permitted to do so.

[3] Communications authorized by law include communications in the course of investigative activities of attorneys representing governmental entities, directly or through investigative agents, before the commencement of criminal or civil enforcement proceedings if there is applicable judicial precedent holding either that the activity is permissible or that the Rule does not apply to the activity. The term "civil enforcement proceedings" includes administrative

enforcement proceedings. Except to the extent applicable judicial precedent holds otherwise, a government attorney who communicates with a represented criminal defendant must comply with this Rule.

[4] An attorney who is uncertain whether a communication with a represented person is permissible may seek a court order in exceptional circumstances. For example, when a represented criminal defendant expresses a desire to speak to the prosecutor without the knowledge of the defendant's attorney, the prosecutor may seek a court order appointing substitute an attorney to represent the defendant with respect to the communication.

[5] This Rule applies to communications with any person, whether or not a party to a formal adjudicative proceeding, contract, or negotiation, who is represented by an attorney concerning the matter to which the communication relates. The Rule applies even though the represented person initiates or consents to the communication. An attorney must immediately terminate communication with a person if, after commencing communication, the attorney learns that the person is one with whom communication is not permitted by this Rule.

[6] If an agent or employee of a represented person that is an organization is represented in the matter by the agent or employee's own attorney, the consent by that attorney to a communication will be sufficient for purposes of this Rule. Compare Rule 19–303.4 (f) (3.4). In communicating with a current agent or employee of an organization, an attorney must not seek to obtain information that the attorney knows or reasonably should know is subject to an evidentiary or other privilege of the organization. Consent of the organization's attorney is not required for communication with a former employee. Regarding communications with former employees, see Rule 19–304.4 (c) (4.4).

[7] The prohibition on communications with a represented person applies only if the attorney has actual knowledge that the person in fact is represented in the matter to be discussed. Actual knowledge may be inferred from the circumstances. The attorney cannot evade

the requirement of obtaining the consent of the opposing attorney by ignoring the obvious.

[8] Rule 19–304.3 (4.3) applies to a communication by an attorney with a person not known to be represented by an attorney.

[9] Section (c) of this Rule recognizes that special considerations come into play when an attorney is seeking to redress grievances involving the government. Subject to certain conditions, it permits communications with those in government having the authority to redress the grievances (but not with any other government personnel) without the prior consent of the attorney representing the government in the matter. Section (c) of this Rule does not, however, permit an attorney to bypass attorneys representing the government on every issue that may arise in the course of disputes with the government. Rather, the section provides attorneys with access to decision makers in government with respect to genuine grievances, such as to present the view that the government's basic policy position with respect to a dispute is faulty or that government personnel are conducting themselves improperly with respect to aspects of the dispute. It does not provide direct access on routine disputes, such as ordinary discovery disputes or extensions of time.

♦ ♦ ♦

Model Rules Comparison: This Rule substantially retains Maryland language as it existed prior to the Ethics 2000 Amendments to the ABA Model Rules of Professional Conduct except for dividing Rule 19–304.2 (b) (4.2) into Rule 19–304.2 (b) and (c) (4.2) with no change in wording.

RULE 4.3

DEALING WITH UNREPRESENTED PERSON

An attorney, in dealing on behalf of a client with a person who is not represented by an attorney, shall not state or imply that the attorney is disinterested. When the attorney knows or reasonably should know that the unrepresented person misunderstands the attorney's role in the matter, the attorney shall make reasonable efforts to correct the misunderstanding.

COMMENT

[1] An unrepresented person, particularly one not experienced in dealing with legal matters, might assume that an attorney is disinterested in loyalties or is a disinterested authority on the law even when the attorney represents a client. In order to avoid a misunderstanding, an attorney will typically need to identify the attorney's client and, where necessary, explain that the client has interests opposed to those of the unrepresented person. For misunderstandings that sometimes arise when an attorney for an organization deals with an unrepresented constituent, see Rule 19–301.13 (d) (1.13).

[2] An attorney should not give legal advice to an unrepresented person, other than the advice to secure an attorney, if the attorney knows or reasonably should know that the interests of such a person are or have a reasonable possibility of being in conflict with the interests of the client. This distinguishes between situations involving unrepresented persons whose interests may be adverse to those of the attorney's client and those in which the person's interests are not in conflict with the client's. In the former situation, the possibility that the attorney will compromise the unrepresented person's interests is so great that the attorney should not give any advice, apart from the advice to obtain an attorney. Whether an attorney is giving impermissible advice may depend on the experience and sophistication of the unrepresented person, as well as the setting in which the behavior and comments occur. This Rule does not prohibit an attorney from negotiating the terms of a transaction or settling a dispute with an unrepresented person. So long as the attorney has explained that the attorney represents an adverse party and is not representing the person, the attorney may inform the person of the terms on which the attorney's client will enter into an agreement or settle a matter, prepare documents that require the person's signature and explain the attorney's own view of the meaning of the document or the attorney's view of the underlying legal obligations.

♦ ♦ ♦

Model Rules Comparison: Rule 19–304.3 (4.3) has been rewritten to retain elements of existing Maryland language, to incorporate some changes from the Ethics 2000 Amendments to the ABA Model Rules, and to incorporate further revisions.

RULE 4.4

RESPECT FOR RIGHTS OF THIRD PERSONS

(a) In representing a client, an attorney shall not use means that have no substantial purpose other than to embarrass, delay, or burden a third person, or use methods of obtaining evidence that violate the legal rights of such a person.

(b) An attorney who receives a document, electronically stored information, or other property relating to the representation of the attorney's client and knows or reasonably should know that the document, electronically stored information, or other property was inadvertently sent shall promptly notify the sender.

(c) In communicating with third persons, an attorney representing a client in a matter shall not seek information relating to the matter that the attorney knows or reasonably should know is protected from disclosure by statute or by an established evidentiary privilege, unless the protection has been waived. An attorney who receives information that is protected from disclosure shall (1) terminate the communication immediately and (2) give notice of the disclosure to the person entitled to enforce the protection against disclosure. If the person entitled to enforce the protection against disclosure is represented by an attorney, the notice required by this Rule shall be given to the person's attorney.

COMMENT

[1] Responsibility to a client requires an attorney to subordinate the interests of others to those of the client, but that responsibility does not imply that an attorney may disregard the rights of third persons. It is impractical to catalogue all such rights, but they include legal restrictions on methods of obtaining evidence from third persons

and unwarranted intrusions into privileged relationships, such as the client-attorney relationship.

[2] Section (b) recognizes that attorneys sometimes receive a document, electronically stored information, or other property that was inadvertently sent or produced by opposing parties or their attorneys. A document, electronically stored information, or other property is inadvertently sent when it is accidentally transmitted, such as when an email or letter is misaddressed or a document, electronically stored information, or other property is accidentally included with information that was intentionally transmitted. If an attorney knows or reasonably should know that such a document, electronically stored information, or other property was sent inadvertently, this Rule requires the attorney promptly to notify the sender in order to permit that person to take protective measures. Whether the attorney is required to take additional steps, such as returning the document, electronically stored information, or other property, is a matter of law beyond the scope of these Rules, as is the question of whether the privileged status of a document, electronically stored information, or other property has been waived. Similarly, this Rule does not address the legal duties of an attorney who receives a document, electronically stored information, or other property that the attorney knows or reasonably should know may have been inappropriately obtained by the sending person. For purposes of this Rule, "document, electronically stored information, or other property" includes, in addition to paper documents, email and other forms of electronically stored information, including embedded data(commonly referred to as "metadata"), that is subject to being read or put into readable form. Metadata in electronic documents creates an obligation under this Rule only if the receiving attorney knows or reasonably should know that the metadata was inadvertently sent to the receiving attorney.

[3] Some attorneys may choose to return a document or delete electronically stored information unread, for example, when the attorney learns before receiving it that it was inadvertently sent. Where an attorney is not required by applicable law to do so, the decision to voluntarily return such a document or delete

electronically stored information is a matter of professional judgment ordinarily reserved to the attorney. See Rules 19–301.2 and 19–301.4.

[4] Third persons may possess information that is confidential to another person under an evidentiary privilege or under a law providing specific confidentiality protection, such as trademark, copyright, or patent law. For example, present or former organizational employees or agents may have information that is protected as a privileged attorney-client communication or as work product. An attorney may not knowingly seek to obtain confidential information from a person who the attorney knows or reasonably should know has no authority to waive the privilege. Regarding current employees of a represented organization, see also Rule 19–304.2 (4.2).

♦ ♦ ♦

Model Rules Comparison—Sections (a) and (b) of Rule 19–304.4 are substantially similar to the language of Model Rule 4.4 of the Ethics 2000 amendments to the ABA Model Rules of Professional Conduct. Section (c) substantially restores to the Rule Maryland language as it existed prior to a 2017 amendment, with slight modification.

Cross reference: To compare generally the duties of a party who receives inadvertently sent materials during discovery in a civil action in a circuit court, see Rule 2–402. See also Rules 2–510 and 2–510.1 to compare the duties of a party who receives inadvertently sent materials in answer to a subpoena. See Rules 1–331 and 19–304.2 (4.2) concerning communications with a person represented by an attorney.

FIRMS AND ASSOCIATIONS

RULE 5.1

RESPONSIBILITIES OF PARTNERS, MANAGERS, AND SUPERVISORY LAWYERS

(a) A partner in a law firm, and an attorney who individually or together with other attorneys possesses comparable managerial authority in a law firm, shall make reasonable efforts to ensure that the firm has in effect measures giving reasonable assurance that all attorneys in the firm conform to the Maryland Attorneys' Rules of Professional Conduct.

(b) An attorney having direct supervisory authority over another attorney shall make reasonable efforts to ensure that the other attorney conforms to the Maryland Attorneys' Rules of Professional Conduct.

(c) An attorney shall be responsible for another attorney's violation of the Maryland Attorneys' Rules of Professional Conduct if:

(1) the attorney orders or, with knowledge of the specific conduct, ratifies the conduct involved; or

(2) the attorney is a partner or has comparable managerial authority in the law firm in which the other attorney practices, or has direct supervisory authority over the other attorney, and knows of the conduct at a time when its consequences can be avoided or mitigated but fails to take reasonable remedial action.

COMMENT

[1] Section (a) of this Rule applies to attorneys who have managerial authority over the professional work of a firm. See Rule 19–301.0 (e) (1.0). This includes members of a partnership, the shareholders in a law firm organized as a professional corporation, and members of other associations authorized to practice law; attorneys having comparable managerial authority in a legal services organization or a law department of an enterprise or government agency; and attorneys who have intermediate managerial responsibilities in a firm. Section (b) of this Rule applies to attorneys who have supervisory authority over the work of other attorneys in a firm.

[2] Section (a) of this Rule requires attorneys with managerial authority within a firm to make reasonable efforts to establish internal policies and procedures designed to provide reasonable assurance that all attorneys in the firm will conform to the Maryland Attorneys' Rules of Professional Conduct. Such policies and procedures include those designed to detect and resolve conflicts of interest, identify dates by which actions must be taken in pending matters, account for client funds and property and ensure that inexperienced attorneys are properly supervised.

[3] Other measures that may be required to fulfill the responsibility prescribed in section (a) of this Rule can depend on the firm's structure and the nature of its practice. In a small firm of experienced attorneys, informal supervision and periodic review of compliance with the required systems ordinarily will suffice. In a large firm, or in practice situations in which difficult ethical problems frequently arise, more elaborate measures may be necessary. Some firms, for example, have a procedure whereby junior attorneys can make confidential referral of ethical problems directly to a designated senior partner or special committee. See Rule 19–305.2 (5.2). Firms, whether large or small, may also rely on continuing legal education in professional ethics. In any event, the ethical atmosphere of a firm can influence the conduct of all its members and the partners may not assume that all attorneys associated with the firm will inevitably conform to the Rules.

[4] Section (c) of this Rule expresses a general principle of personal responsibility for acts of another. See also Rule 19–308.4 (a) (8.4).

[5] Subsection (c)(2) of this Rule defines the duty of a partner or other attorney having comparable managerial authority in a law firm, as well as an attorney who has direct supervisory authority over performance of specific legal work by another attorney. Whether an attorney has supervisory authority in particular circumstances is a question of fact. Partners and attorneys with comparable authority have at least indirect responsibility for all work being done by the firm, while a partner or manager in charge of a particular matter ordinarily also has supervisory responsibility for the work of other firm attorneys engaged in the matter. Appropriate remedial action by a partner or managing attorney would depend on the immediacy of that attorney's involvement and the seriousness of the misconduct. A supervisor is required to intervene to prevent avoidable consequences of misconduct if the supervisor knows that the misconduct occurred. Thus, if a supervising attorney knows that a subordinate misrepresented a matter to an opposing party in negotiation, the supervisor as well as the subordinate has a duty to correct the resulting misapprehension.

[6] Professional misconduct by an attorney under supervision could reveal a violation of section (b) of this Rule on the part of the supervisory attorney even though it does not entail a violation of section (c) of this Rule because there was no direction, ratification or knowledge of the violation.

[7] Apart from this Rule and Rule 19–308.4 (a) (8.4), an attorney does not have disciplinary liability for the conduct of a partner, associate or subordinate. Whether an attorney may be liable civilly or criminally for another attorney's conduct is a question of law beyond the scope of these Rules.

[8] The duties imposed by this Rule on managing and supervising attorneys do not alter the personal duty of each attorney in a firm to abide by the Maryland Attorneys' Rules of Professional Conduct. See Rule 19–305.2 (a) (5.2).

♦ ♦ ♦

Model Rules Comparison: Rule 19–305.1 (5.1) is substantially similar to the language of the Ethics 2000 Amendments to the ABA Model Rules of Professional Conduct.

RULE 5.2

Responsibilities of a Subordinate Lawyer

(a) An attorney is bound by the Maryland Attorneys' Rules of Professional Conduct notwithstanding that the attorney acted at the direction of another person.

(b) A subordinate attorney does not violate the Maryland Attorneys' Rules of Professional Conduct if that attorney acts in accordance with a supervisory attorney's reasonable resolution of an arguable question of professional duty.

COMMENT

[1] Although an attorney is not relieved of responsibility for a violation by the fact that the attorney acted at the direction of a supervisor, that fact may be relevant in determining whether an attorney had the knowledge required to render conduct a violation of the Rules. For example, if a subordinate filed a frivolous pleading at

the direction of a supervisor, the subordinate would not be guilty of a professional violation unless the subordinate knew of the document's frivolous character.

[2] When attorneys in a supervisor-subordinate relationship encounter a matter involving professional judgment as to ethical duty, the supervisor may assume responsibility for making the judgment. Otherwise a consistent course of action or position could not be taken. If the question can reasonably be answered only one way, the duty of both attorneys is clear and they are equally responsible for fulfilling it. However, if the question is reasonably arguable, someone has to decide upon the course of action. That authority ordinarily reposes in the supervisor, and a subordinate may be guided accordingly. For example, if a question arises whether the interests of two clients conflict under Rule 19–301.7 (1.7), the supervisor's reasonable resolution of the question should protect the subordinate professionally if the resolution is subsequently challenged.

♦ ♦ ♦

Model Rules Comparison: Given that the Ethics 2000 Amendments to the ABA Model Rules of Professional Conduct made no changes to this Rule, Rule 19–305.2 (5.2) has not been amended and remains substantially similar to Model Rule 5.2.

RULE 5.3

RESPONSIBILITIES REGARDING NONLAWYER ASSISTANTS

With respect to a non-attorney employed or retained by or associated with an attorney:

(a) a partner, and an attorney who individually or together with other attorneys possesses comparable managerial authority in a law firm shall make reasonable efforts to ensure that the firm has in effect measures giving reasonable assurance that the person's conduct is compatible with the professional obligations of the attorney;

(b) an attorney having direct supervisory authority over the non-attorney shall make reasonable efforts to ensure that the person's conduct is compatible with the professional obligations of the attorney;

(c) an attorney shall be responsible for conduct of such a person that would be a violation of the Maryland Attorneys' Rules of Professional Conduct if engaged in by an attorney if:

   (1) the attorney orders or, with the knowledge of the specific conduct, ratifies the conduct involved; or

   (2) the attorney is a partner or has comparable managerial authority in the law firm in which the person is employed, or has direct supervisory authority over the person, and knows of the conduct at a time when its consequences can be avoided or mitigated but fails to take reasonable remedial action; and

(d) an attorney who employs or retains the services of a non-attorney who (1) was formerly admitted to the practice of law in any jurisdiction and (2) has been and remains disbarred, suspended, or placed on inactive status because of incapacity shall comply with the following requirements:

   (A) all law-related activities of the formerly admitted attorney shall be (i) performed from an office that is staffed on a full-time basis by a supervising attorney and (ii) conducted under the direct supervision of the supervising attorney, who shall be responsible for ensuring that the formerly admitted attorney complies with the requirements of this Rule.

   (B) the attorney shall take reasonable steps to ensure that the formerly admitted attorney does not:

      (i) represent himself or herself to be an attorney;

      (ii) render legal consultation or advice to a client or prospective client;

      (iii) appear on behalf of or represent a client in any judicial, administrative, legislative, or alternative dispute resolution proceeding;

      (iv) appear on behalf of or represent a client at a deposition or in any other discovery matter;

      (v) negotiate or transact any matter on behalf of a client with third parties;

(vi) receive funds from or on behalf of a client or disburse funds to or on behalf of a client; or

(vii) perform any law-related activity for (a) a law firm or attorney with whom the formerly admitted attorney was associated when the acts that resulted in the disbarment or suspension occurred or (b) any client who was previously represented by the formerly admitted attorney.

(C) the attorney, the supervising attorney, and the formerly admitted attorney shall file jointly with Bar Counsel (i) a notice of employment identifying the supervising attorney and the formerly admitted attorney and listing each jurisdiction in which the formerly admitted attorney has been disbarred, suspended, or placed on inactive status because of incapacity; and (ii) a copy of an executed written agreement between the attorney, the supervising attorney, and the formerly admitted attorney that sets forth the duties of the formerly admitted attorney and includes an undertaking to comply with requests by Bar Counsel for proof of compliance with the terms of the agreement and this Rule. As to a formerly admitted attorney employed as of July 1, 2006, the notice and agreement shall be filed no later than September 1, 2006. As to a formerly admitted attorney hired after July 1, 2006, the notice and agreement shall be filed within 30 days after commencement of the employment. Immediately upon the termination of the employment of the formerly admitted attorney, the attorney and the supervising attorney shall file with Bar Counsel a notice of the termination.

COMMENT

[1] Attorneys generally employ assistants in their practice, including secretaries, investigators, law student interns, and paraprofessionals. Such assistants, whether employees or independent contractors, act for the attorney in rendition of the attorney's professional services. An attorney must give such assistants appropriate instruction and supervision concerning the ethical aspects of their employment, particularly regarding the obligation not to disclose

information relating to representation of the client, and should be responsible for their work product. The measures employed in supervising non-attorneys should take account of the fact that they do not have legal training and are not subject to professional discipline.

[2] Section (a) of this Rule requires attorneys with managerial authority within a law firm to make reasonable efforts to establish internal policies and procedures designed to provide reasonable assurance that non-attorneys in the firm will act in a way compatible with the Maryland Attorneys' Rules of Professional Conduct. See Comment [1] to Rule 19–305.1 (5.1). Section (b) of this Rule applies to attorneys who have supervisory authority over the work of a non-attorney. Section (c) of this Rule specifies the circumstances in which an attorney is responsible for conduct of a non-attorney that would be a violation of the Maryland Attorneys' Rules of Professional Conduct if engaged in by an attorney.

[3] Section (d) of this Rule addresses formerly admitted attorneys engaging in law-related activities and does not establish a standard for what constitutes the unauthorized practice of law.

♦ ♦ ♦

Model Rules Comparison: The language of Rule 19–305.3 (a) through (c) (5.3) is substantially similar to the language of the Ethics 2000 Amendments to the ABA Model Rules of Professional Conduct. Section (d) of this Rule and Comment [3] are in part derived from Rule 217 (j) of the Pennsylvania Rules of Disciplinary Enforcement and in part new.

RULE 5.4

PROFESSIONAL INDEPENDENCE OF A LAWYER

(a) An attorney or law firm shall not share legal fees with a non-attorney, except that:

(1) an agreement by an attorney with the attorney's firm, partner, or associate may provide for the payment of money, over a reasonable period of time after the attorney's death, to the attorney's estate or to one or more specified persons;

(2) an attorney who purchases the practice of an attorney who is deceased or disabled or who has disappeared may, pursuant to the provisions of Rule 19–301.17 (1.17), pay the purchase price to the estate or representative of the attorney.

(3) an attorney who undertakes to complete unfinished legal business of a deceased, retired, disabled, or suspended attorney may pay to that attorney or that attorney's estate the proportion of the total compensation fairly allocable to the services rendered by the former attorney;

(4) an attorney or law firm may include non-attorney employees in a compensation or retirement plan, even though the plan is based in whole or in part on a profit-sharing arrangement; and

(5) an attorney may share court-awarded legal fees with a non-profit organization that employed, retained or recommended employment of the attorney in the matter.

(b) An attorney shall not form a partnership with a non-attorney if any of the activities of the partnership consist of the practice of law.

(c) An attorney shall not permit a person who recommends, employs, or pays the attorney to render legal services for another to direct or regulate the attorney's professional judgment in rendering such legal services.

(d) An attorney shall not practice with or in the form of a professional corporation or association authorized to practice law for a profit, if:

(1) a non-attorney owns any interest therein, except that a fiduciary representative of the estate of an attorney may hold the stock or interest of the attorney for a reasonable time during administration;

(2) a non-attorney is a corporate director or officer thereof or occupies the position of similar responsibility in any form of association other than a corporation; or

(3) a non-attorney has the right to direct or control the professional judgment of an attorney.

♦ ♦ ♦

Cross reference: Md. Rule 19–741.

COMMENT

[1] The provisions of this Rule express traditional limitations on sharing fees. These limitations are to protect the attorney's professional independence of judgment. Where someone other than the client pays the attorney's fee or salary, or recommends employment of the attorney, that arrangement does not modify the attorney's obligation to the client. As stated in section (c) of this Rule, such arrangements should not interfere with the attorney's professional judgment.

[2] This Rule also expresses traditional limitations on permitting a third party to direct or regulate the attorney's professional judgment in rendering legal services to another. See also Rule 19–301.8 (f) (1.8) (attorney may accept compensation from a third party as long as there is no interference with the attorney's independent professional judgment and the client gives informed consent).

♦ ♦ ♦

Model Rules Comparison: Rule 19–305.4 (5.4) is substantially similar to the language of the Ethics 2000 Amendments to the ABA Model Rules of Professional Conduct with the exception of: 1) retaining existing Maryland language in Rule 19–305.4 (a)(2) (5.4); 2) retaining existing Maryland language in Rule 19–305.4 (a)(3) (5.4) with appropriate redesignation of the subsections of Rule 19–305.4 (a) (5.4).

RULE 5.5

UNAUTHORIZED PRACTICE OF LAW; MULTIJURISDICTIONAL PRACTICE OF LAW

(a) An attorney shall not practice law in a jurisdiction in violation of the regulation of the legal profession in that jurisdiction, or assist another in doing so.

(b) An attorney who is not admitted to practice in this jurisdiction shall not:

(1) except as authorized by these Rules or other law, establish an office or other systematic and continuous presence in this jurisdiction for the practice of law; or

(2) hold out to the public or otherwise represent that the attorney is admitted to practice law in this jurisdiction.

(c) An attorney admitted in another United States jurisdiction, and not disbarred or suspended from practice in any jurisdiction, may provide legal services on a temporary basis in this jurisdiction that:

(1) are undertaken in association with an attorney who is admitted to practice in this jurisdiction and who actively participates in the matter;

(2) are in or reasonably related to a pending or potential proceeding before a tribunal in this or another jurisdiction, if the attorney, or a person the attorney is assisting, is authorized by law or order to appear in such proceeding or reasonably expects to be so authorized;

(3) are in or reasonably related to a pending or potential arbitration, mediation, or other alternative dispute resolution proceeding in this or another jurisdiction, if the services arise out of or are reasonably related to the attorney's practice in a jurisdiction in which the attorney is admitted to practice and are not services for which the forum requires pro hac vice admission; or

(4) are not within subsections (c)(2) or (c)(3) of this Rule and arise out of or are reasonably related to the attorney's practice in a jurisdiction in which the attorney is admitted to practice.

(d) An attorney admitted in another United States jurisdiction, and not disbarred or suspended from practice in any jurisdiction, may provide legal services in this jurisdiction and may establish an office or other systematic or continuous presence in this jurisdiction to provide those services if the legal services

(1) are provided to the attorney's employer or its organizational affiliates and are not services for which the forum requires pro hac vice admission;

(2) are services that the attorney is authorized to provide by federal law or other law of this jurisdiction; or

(3) exclusively involve the law of another jurisdiction in which the attorney is licensed to practice law, provided the attorney advises the attorney's client in writing that the attorney is not licensed to practice Maryland law.

(e)

(1) In this section, "foreign attorney" means an attorney who (A) is not admitted to practice law in any United States jurisdiction, (B) is a member in good standing of a recognized legal profession in a country other than the United States and, as such, is authorized to practice law in that country, (C) is subject to effective regulation and discipline by a duly constituted professional body or a public authority of that country, and (D) has not been disbarred or suspended from the practice of law in any jurisdiction of the United States.

(2) A foreign attorney may not establish an office or other systematic and continuous presence in this State for the practice of law, or hold out to the public or otherwise represent that the attorney is admitted to practice law in this State. Any violation of this provision or any material misrepresentation regarding the requirements in subsection (e)(1) of this Rule by the foreign attorney will subject the foreign attorney to liability for the unauthorized practice of law.

(3) A foreign attorney, with respect to any matter, may (A) act as a consultant to a Maryland attorney on the law and practice in a country in which the foreign attorney is admitted to practice, including principles of international law recognized and enforced in that country and (B) in association with a Maryland attorney who actively participates in the matter, participate in discussions with a client of the Maryland attorney or with other persons involved with the matter, provided that the Maryland attorney shall remain fully responsible to the client for all advice and other conduct by the foreign attorney with respect to the matter.

COMMENT

[1] An attorney may practice law only in a jurisdiction in which the attorney is authorized to practice. An attorney may be admitted to practice law in a jurisdiction on a regular basis or may be authorized by court rule or order or by law to practice for a limited purpose or

on a restricted basis. Section (a) of this Rule applies to unauthorized practice of law by an attorney, whether through the attorney's direct action or by the attorney's assisting another person.

[2] The definition of the practice of law is established by law and varies from one jurisdiction to another. Whatever the definition, limiting the practice of law to members of the bar protects the public against rendition of legal services by unqualified persons. This Rule does not prohibit an attorney from employing the services of paraprofessionals and delegating functions to them, so long as the attorney supervises the delegated work and retains responsibility for their work. See Rule 19–305.3 (5.3).

[3] An attorney may provide professional advice and instruction to non-attorneys whose employment requires knowledge of law; for example, claims adjusters, employees of financial or commercial institutions, social workers, accountants and individuals employed in government agencies. Attorneys also may assist independent non-attorneys, such as paraprofessionals, who are authorized by the law of a jurisdiction to provide particular law-related services. In addition, an attorney may counsel non- attorneys who wish to proceed self-represented.

[4] Other than as authorized by law or this Rule, an attorney who is not admitted to practice generally in this jurisdiction violates section (b) of this Rule if the attorney establishes an office or other systematic and continuous presence in this jurisdiction for the practice of law. Presence may be systematic and continuous even if the attorney is not physically present here. Such an attorney must not hold out to the public or otherwise represent that the attorney is admitted to practice law in this jurisdiction. See also Rules 19–307.1 (a) (7.1) and 19–307.5 (b) (7.5).

[5] There are occasions in which an attorney admitted to practice in another United States jurisdiction, and not disbarred or suspended from practice in any jurisdiction, may provide legal services on a temporary basis in this jurisdiction under circumstances that do not create an unreasonable risk to the interests of their clients, the public or the courts. Section (c) of this Rule identifies four such

circumstances. The fact that conduct is not so identified does not imply that the conduct is or is not authorized.

[6] There is no single test to determine whether an attorney's services are provided on a "temporary basis" in this jurisdiction, and may therefore be permissible under section (c) of this Rule. Services may be "temporary" even though the attorney provides services in this jurisdiction on a recurring basis, or for an extended period of time, as when the attorney is representing a client in a single lengthy negotiation or litigation.

[7] Sections (c) and (d) of this Rule apply to attorneys who are admitted to practice law in any United States jurisdiction, which includes the District of Columbia and any state, territory or commonwealth of the United States. The word "admitted" in section (c) of this Rule contemplates that the attorney is authorized to practice in the jurisdiction in which the attorney is admitted and excludes an attorney who while technically admitted is not authorized to practice, because, for example, the attorney is on inactive status.

[8] Subsection (c)(1) of this Rule recognizes that the interests of clients and the public are protected if an attorney admitted only in another jurisdiction associates with an attorney licensed to practice in this jurisdiction. For this subsection to apply, however, the attorney admitted to practice in this jurisdiction must actively participate in and share responsibility for the representation of the client.

[9] Attorneys not admitted to practice generally in a jurisdiction may be authorized by law or order of a tribunal or an administrative agency to appear before the tribunal or agency. This authority may be granted pursuant to formal rules governing admission pro hac vice or pursuant to informal practice of the tribunal or agency. Under subsection (c)(2) of this Rule, an attorney does not violate this Rule when the attorney appears before a tribunal or agency pursuant to such authority. An attorney who is not admitted to practice in this jurisdiction must obtain admission pro hac vice before appearing before a tribunal or administrative agency, as provided by Rule 19–214 of the Rules Governing Admission to the Bar of

Maryland. See also Md. Code, Business Occupations and Professions Article, § 10–215.

[10] Subsection (c)(2) of this Rule also provides that an attorney rendering services in this jurisdiction on a temporary basis does not violate this Rule when the attorney engages in conduct in anticipation of a proceeding or hearing in a jurisdiction in which the attorney is authorized to practice law or in which the attorney reasonably expects to be admitted pro hac vice. Examples of such conduct include meetings with the client, interviews of potential witnesses, and the review of documents. Similarly, an attorney admitted only in another jurisdiction may engage in conduct temporarily in this jurisdiction in connection with pending litigation in another jurisdiction in which the attorney is or reasonably expects to be authorized to appear, including taking depositions in this jurisdiction.

[11] When an attorney has been or reasonably expects to be admitted to appear before a court or administrative agency, subsection (c)(2) of this Rule also permits conduct by attorneys who are associated with that attorney in the matter, but who do not expect to appear before the court or administrative agency. For example, subordinate attorneys may conduct research, review documents, and attend meetings with witnesses in support of the attorney responsible for the litigation.

[12] Subsection (c)(3) of this Rule permits an attorney admitted to practice law in another jurisdiction to perform services on a temporary basis in this jurisdiction if those services are in or reasonably related to a pending or potential arbitration, mediation, or other alternative dispute resolution proceeding in this or another jurisdiction, if the services arise out of or are reasonably related to the attorney's practice in a jurisdiction in which the attorney is admitted to practice. The attorney, however, must obtain permission pro hac vice in the case of a court-annexed arbitration or mediation or otherwise if court rules or law so require. See Rule 19–214 of the Rules Governing Admission to the Bar of Maryland regarding admission to appear in arbitrations.

[13] Subsection (c)(4) of this Rule permits an attorney admitted in another jurisdiction to provide certain legal services on a temporary

basis in this jurisdiction that arise out of or are reasonably related to the attorney's practice in a jurisdiction in which the attorney is admitted but are not within subsections (c)(2) or (c)(3) of this Rule. These services include both legal services and services that non-attorneys may perform but that are considered the practice of law when performed by attorneys.

[14] Subsections (c)(3) and (c)(4) of this Rule require that the services arise out of or be reasonably related to the attorney's practice in a jurisdiction in which the attorney is admitted. A variety of factors evidence such a relationship. The attorney's client may have been previously represented by the attorney, or may be resident in or have substantial contacts with the jurisdiction in which the attorney is admitted. The matter, although involving other jurisdictions, may have a significant connection with that jurisdiction. In other cases, significant aspects of the attorney's work might be conducted in that jurisdiction or a significant aspect of the matter may involve the law of that jurisdiction. The necessary relationship might arise when the client's activities or the legal issues involve multiple jurisdictions, such as when the officers of a multinational corporation survey potential business sites and seek the services of their attorney in assessing the relative merits of each. In addition, the services may draw on the attorney's recognized expertise developed through the regular practice of law on behalf of clients in matters involving a particular body of federal, nationally-uniform, foreign, or international law.

[15] Section (d) of this Rule identifies three circumstances in which an attorney who is admitted to practice in another United States jurisdiction, and is not disbarred or suspended from practice in any jurisdiction, may establish an office or other systematic and continuous presence in this jurisdiction for the practice of law as well as provide legal services on a temporary basis.

[16] Subsection (d)(1) of this Rule applies to an attorney who is employed by a client to provide legal services to the client or its organizational affiliates, i.e., entities that control, are controlled by, or are under common control with the employer. This subsection does not authorize the provision of personal legal services to the

employer's officers or employees. The subsection applies to in-house corporate attorneys, government attorneys and others who are employed to render legal services to the employer. The attorney's ability to represent the employer outside the jurisdiction in which the attorney is licensed generally serves the interests of the employer and does not create an unreasonable risk to the client and others because the employer is well situated to assess the attorney's qualifications and the quality of the attorney's work.

[17] If an employed attorney establishes an office or other systematic presence in this jurisdiction for the purpose of rendering legal services to the employer, the attorney is governed by Md. Code, Business Occupations and Professions Article, § 1–206(d). In general, the employed attorney is subject to disciplinary proceedings under the Maryland Rules and must comply with Md. Code, Business Occupations and Professions Article, § 10–215 (and Rule 19–214) for authorization to appear before a tribunal. See also Rule 19–215 (as to legal services attorneys).

[18] Subsection (d)(2) of this Rule recognizes that an attorney may provide legal services in a jurisdiction in which the attorney is not licensed when authorized to do so by federal or other law, which includes statute, court rule, executive regulation or judicial precedent. Subsection (d)(3) recognizes that an attorney who is not licensed in Maryland may provide legal services in Maryland if the services exclusively involve the law of another jurisdiction in which the attorney is licensed to practice. The attorney must advise the client in writing that the attorney is not licensed to practice Maryland law. *See Attorney Grievance Commission v. Jackson*, 477 Md. 174 (2022).

[19] An attorney who practices law in this jurisdiction pursuant to section (c) or (d) of this Rule or otherwise is subject to the disciplinary authority of this jurisdiction. See Rule 19–308.5 (a) (8.5) and Md. Rules 19–701 and 19–711.

[20] In some circumstances, an attorney who practices law in this jurisdiction pursuant to section (c) or (d) of this Rule may have to inform the client that the attorney is not licensed to practice law in this jurisdiction. For example, that may be required when the representation

occurs primarily in this jurisdiction and requires knowledge of the law of this jurisdiction. See Rule 19–301.4 (b) (1.4).

[21] Sections (c) and (d) of this Rule do not authorize communications advertising legal services to prospective clients in this jurisdiction by attorneys who are admitted to practice in other jurisdictions. Rules 19–307.1 (7.1) to 19–307.5 (7.5) govern whether and how attorneys may communicate the availability of their services to prospective clients in this jurisdiction.

[22] Section (e) is not intended to permit a foreign attorney to be admitted *pro hac vice* in any proceeding, but it does not preclude the foreign attorney (1) from being present with a Maryland attorney at a judicial, administrative, or ADR proceeding to provide consultative services to the Maryland attorney during the proceeding, or (2) subject to Rule 5–702, from testifying as an expert witness.

♦ ♦ ♦

Model Rules Comparison: Rule 19–305.5 (5.5) is substantially similar to the language of the Ethics 2000 Amendments to the ABA Model Rules of Professional Conduct, except that subsection (d)(3) and section (e) are new.

RULE 5.6

RESTRICTIONS ON RIGHT TO PRACTICE

An attorney shall not participate in offering or making:

(a) a partnership, shareholders, operating, employment, or other similar type of agreement that restricts the right of an attorney to practice after termination of the relationship, except an agreement concerning benefits upon retirement; or

(b) an agreement in which a restriction on the attorney's right to practice is part of the settlement of a client controversy.

COMMENT

[1] An agreement restricting the right of attorneys to practice after leaving a firm not only limits their professional autonomy but also limits the freedom of clients to choose an attorney. Section (a) of this Rule prohibits such agreement except for restrictions

incident to provisions concerning retirement benefits for service with the firm.

[2] Section (b) of this Rule prohibits an attorney from agreeing not to represent other persons in connection with settling a claim on behalf of a client.

[3] This Rule does not apply to prohibit restrictions that may be included in the terms of the sale of a law practice pursuant to Rule 19–301.17 (1.17).

♦ ♦ ♦

Model Rules Comparison: Rule 19–305.6 (5.6) is substantially similar to the language of the Ethics 2000 Amendments to the ABA Model Rules of Professional Conduct.

RULE 5.7

RESPONSIBILITIES REGARDING LAW-RELATED SERVICES

(a) An attorney shall be subject to the Maryland Attorneys' Rules of Professional Conduct with respect to the provision of law- related services, as defined in section (b) of this Rule, if the law-related services are provided:

  (1) by the attorney in circumstances that are not distinct from the attorney's provision of legal services to clients; or

  (2) in other circumstances by an entity controlled by the attorney individually or with others if the attorney fails to take reasonable measures to assure that a person obtaining the law-related services knows that the services are not legal services and that the protections of the client-attorney relationship do not exist.

(b) The term "law-related services" denotes services that might reasonably be performed in conjunction with and in substance are related to the provision of legal services, and that are not prohibited as unauthorized practice of law when provided by a non-attorney.

COMMENT

[1] When an attorney performs law-related services or controls an organization that does so, there exists the potential for ethical problems. Principal among these is the possibility that the person for

whom the law-related services are performed fails to understand that the services may not carry with them the protections normally afforded as part of the client-attorney relationship. The recipient of the law-related services may expect, for example, that the protection of client confidences, prohibitions against representation of persons with conflicting interests, and obligations of an attorney to maintain professional independence apply to the provision of law-related services when that may not be the case.

[2] Rule 19–305.7 (5.7) applies to the provision of law-related services by an attorney even when the attorney does not provide any legal services to the person for whom the law-related services are performed and whether the law-related services are performed through a law firm or a separate entity. The Rule identifies the circumstances in which all of the Maryland Attorneys' Rules of Professional Conduct apply to the provision of law-related services. Even when those circumstances do not exist, however, the conduct of a attorney involved in the provision of law-related services is subject to those Rules that apply generally to attorney conduct, regardless of whether the conduct involves the provision of legal services. See, e.g., Rule 19–308.4 (8.4).

[3] When law-related services are provided by an attorney under circumstances that are not distinct from the attorney's provision of legal services to clients, the attorney in providing the law-related services must adhere to the requirements of the Maryland Attorneys' Rules of Professional Conduct as provided in subsection (a)(1) of this Rule. Even when the law-related and legal services are provided in circumstances that are distinct from each other, for example through separate entities or different support staff within the law firm, the Maryland Attorneys' Rules of Professional Conduct apply to the attorney as provided in subsection (a)(2) of this Rule unless the attorney takes reasonable measures to assure that the recipient of the law-related services knows that the services are not legal services and that the protections of the client-attorney relationship do not apply.

[4] Law-related services also may be provided through an entity that is distinct from that through which the attorney provides legal

services. If the attorney individually or with others has control of such an entity's operations, the Rule requires the attorney to take reasonable measures to assure that each person using the services of the entity knows that the services provided by the entity are not legal services and that the Maryland Attorneys' Rules of Professional Conduct that relate to the client-attorney relationship do not apply. An attorney's control of an entity extends to the ability to direct its operation. Whether an attorney has such control will depend upon the circumstances of the particular case.

[5] An attorney is not required to comply with Rule 19–301.8 (a) (1.8) when referring a person to a separate law-related entity owned or controlled by the attorney for the purpose of providing services to the person. If the attorney also is providing legal services to the person, the attorney must exercise independent professional judgment in making the referral. See Rule 19–302.1 (2.1). Moreover, the attorney must explain the matter to the person to the extent necessary for the person to make an informed decision to accept the attorney's recommendation. See Rule 19–301.4 (b) (1.4).

[6] In taking the reasonable measures referred to in subsection (a) (2) of this Rule to assure that a person using law-related services understands the practical effect or significance of the inapplicability of the Maryland Attorneys' Rules of Professional Conduct, the attorney should communicate to the person receiving the law-related services, in a manner sufficient to assure that the person understands the significance of the fact, that the relationship of the person to the business entity will not be a client- attorney relationship. The communication should be made before entering into an agreement for provision of or providing law- related services, and preferably should be in writing.

[7] The burden is upon the attorney to show that the attorney has taken reasonable measures under the circumstances to communicate the desired understanding. For instance, a sophisticated user of law-related services, such as a publicly held corporation, may require a lesser explanation than someone unaccustomed to making

distinctions between legal services and law-related services, such as an individual seeking tax advice from a attorney-accountant or investigative services in connection with a lawsuit.

[8] Regardless of the sophistication of potential recipients of law-related services, an attorney should take special care to keep separate the provision of law-related and legal services in order to minimize the risk that the recipient will assume that the law-related services are legal services. The risk of such confusion is especially acute when the attorney renders both types of services with respect to the same matter. Under some circumstances the legal and law-related services may be so closely entwined that they cannot be distinguished from each other, and the requirement of disclosure and consultation imposed by subsection (a)(2) of this Rule of the Rule cannot be met. In such a case an attorney will be responsible for assuring that both the attorney's conduct and, to the extent required by Rule 19–305.3 (5.3), that of non-attorney employees in the distinct entity that the attorney complies in all respects with the Maryland Attorneys' Rules of Professional Conduct.

[9] A broad range of economic and other interests of clients may be served by attorneys' engaging in the delivery of law-related services. Examples of law-related services include providing title insurance, financial planning, accounting, trust services, real estate counseling, legislative lobbying, economic analysis, social work, psychological counseling, tax preparation, and patent, medical or environmental consulting.

[10] When an attorney is obliged to accord the recipients of such services the protections of those Rules that apply to the client- attorney relationship, the attorney must take special care to heed the proscriptions of the Rules addressing conflict of interest (Rules 19–301.7 (1.7) through 19–301.11 (1.11), especially Rules 19–301.7 (a)(2) (1.7) and 19–301.8 (b) and (f) (1.8), and to scrupulously adhere to the requirements of Rule 19–301.6 (1.6) relating to disclosure of confidential information. The promotion of the law-related services must also in all respects comply with Rules 19–307.1 (7.1) through 19–307.3 (7.3), dealing with advertising and solicitation. In that regard,

attorneys should take special care to identify the obligations that may be imposed as a result of a jurisdiction's decisional law.

[11] When the full protections of all of the Maryland Attorneys' Rules of Professional Conduct do not apply to the provision of law-related services, principles of law external to the Rules, for example, the law of principal and agent, govern the legal duties owed to those receiving the services. Those other legal principles may establish a different degree of protection for the recipient with respect to confidentiality of information, conflicts of interest and permissible business relationships with clients. See also Rule 19–308.4 (8.4) (Misconduct).

[12] Regarding an attorney's referrals of clients to non-attorney professionals, see Rule 19–307.2 (c) (7.2) and related Comment.

♦ ♦ ♦

Model Rules Comparison: This Rule, newly added to the Model Rules by the Ethics 2000 Amendments to the ABA Model Rules of Professional Conduct, is substantially similar to the ABA Rule, with the exception of changes to Comment [5] and the addition of Comment [12].

PUBLIC SERVICE

RULE 6.1

Pro Bono Publico Service

(a) **Professional Responsibility.** An attorney has a professional responsibility to render pro bono publico legal service.

(b) **Discharge of Professional Responsibility.** An attorney in the full-time practice of law should aspire to render at least 50 hours per year of pro bono publico legal service, and an attorney in part-time practice should aspire to render at least a pro rata number of hours.

(1) Unless an attorney is prohibited by law from rendering the legal services described below, a substantial portion of the applicable hours should be devoted to rendering legal service, without fee or expectation of fee, or at a substantially reduced fee, to:

(A) people of limited means;

(B) charitable, religious, civic, community, governmental, or educational organizations in matters designed primarily to address the needs of people of limited means;

(C) individuals, groups, or organizations seeking to secure or protect civil rights, civil liberties, or public rights; or

(D) charitable, religious, civic, community, governmental, or educational organizations in matters in furtherance of their organizational purposes when the payment of the standard legal fees would significantly deplete the organization's economic resources or would otherwise be inappropriate.

(2) The remainder of the applicable hours may be devoted to activities for improving the law, the legal system, or the legal profession.

(3) An attorney also may discharge the professional responsibility set forth in this Rule by contributing financial support to organizations that provide legal services to persons of limited means.

(c) **Effect of Noncompliance.** This Rule is aspirational, not mandatory. Noncompliance with this Rule shall not be grounds for disciplinary action or other sanctions.

♦ ♦ ♦

Cross reference: For requirements regarding reporting pro bono legal service, see Md. Rule 19–503.

COMMENT

[1] The ABA House of Delegates has formally acknowledged "the basic responsibility of each attorney engaged in the practice of law to provide public interest legal services" without fee, or at a substantially reduced fee, in one or more of the following areas: poverty law, civil rights law, public rights law, charitable organization representation, and the administration of justice. This Rule expresses that policy but is not intended to be enforced through the disciplinary process.

[2] The rights and responsibilities of individuals and organizations in the United States are increasingly defined in legal terms. As a consequence, legal assistance in coping with the web of statutes, rules, and regulations is imperative for persons of modest and limited means, as well as for the relatively well-to-do.

[3] The basic responsibility for providing legal services for those unable to pay ultimately rests upon the individual attorney, and personal involvement in the problems of the disadvantaged can be one of the most rewarding experiences in the life of an attorney. Every attorney, regardless of professional prominence or professional workload, should find time to participate in or otherwise support the provision of legal services to the disadvantaged. The provision of free legal services to those unable to pay reasonable fees continues to be an obligation of each attorney as well as the profession generally, but the efforts of individual attorneys are often not enough to meet the need. Thus, it has been necessary for the profession, the government, and the courts to institute additional programs to provide legal services. Accordingly, legal aid offices, attorney referral services, and other related programs have been developed, and more will be developed by the profession, the government, and the courts. Every attorney should support all proper efforts to meet this need for legal services.

[4] The goal of 50 hours per year for pro bono legal service established in section (b) of this Rule is aspirational; it is a goal, not a requirement. The number used is intended as an average yearly amount over the course of the attorney's career.

[5] An attorney in government service who is prohibited by constitutional, statutory, or regulatory restrictions from performing the pro bono legal services described in subsection (b)(1) of the Rule may discharge the attorney's responsibility by participating in activities described in subsection (b)(2) of this Rule.

♦ ♦ ♦

Model Rules Comparison: This Rule substantially retains Maryland language as amended April 9, 2002, effective July 1, 2002, and does not adopt Ethics 2000 Amendments to the ABA Model Rules of Professional Conduct.

RULE 6.2

ACCEPTING APPOINTMENTS

An attorney shall not seek to avoid appointment by a tribunal to represent a person except for good cause, such as:

(a) representing the client is likely to result in violation of the Maryland Attorneys' Rules of Professional Conduct or other law;

(b) representing the client is likely to result in an unreasonable financial burden on the attorney; or

(c) the client or the cause is so repugnant to the attorney as to be likely to impair the client-attorney relationship or the attorney's ability to represent the client.

COMMENT

[1] An attorney ordinarily is not obliged to accept a client whose character or cause the attorney regards as repugnant. The attorney's freedom to select clients is, however, qualified. All attorneys have a responsibility to assist in providing pro bono publico service. See Rule 19–306.1 (6.1). An individual attorney fulfills this responsibility by accepting a fair share of unpopular matters or indigent or unpopular clients. An attorney may also be subject to appointment by a court to serve unpopular clients or persons unable to afford legal services.

Appointed Attorney

[2] For good cause an attorney may seek to decline an appointment to represent a person who cannot afford to retain an attorney or whose cause is unpopular. Good cause exists if the attorney could not handle the matter competently, see Rule 19–301.1 (1.1), or if undertaking the representation would result in an improper conflict of interest, for example, when the client or the cause is so repugnant to the attorney as to be likely to impair the client-attorney relationship or the attorney's ability to represent the client. An attorney may also seek to decline an appointment if acceptance would be unreasonably burdensome, for example, when it would impose a financial sacrifice so great as to be unjust.

[3] An appointed attorney has the same obligations to the client as a retained attorney, including the obligations of loyalty and confidentiality, and is subject to the same limitations on the client-attorney relationship, such as the obligation to refrain from assisting the client in violation of the Rules.

♦ ♦ ♦

Model Rules Comparison: Given that the Ethics 2000 Amendments to the ABA Model Rules of Professional Conduct made no changes to this Rule, Rule 19–306.2 (6.2) has not been amended and remains substantially similar to Model Rule 6.2.

RULE 6.3

MEMBERSHIP IN LEGAL SERVICES ORGANIZATION

An attorney may serve as a director, officer or member of a legal services organization, apart from the law firm in which the attorney practices, notwithstanding that the organization serves persons having interests adverse to a client of the attorney. The attorney shall not knowingly participate in a decision or action of the organization:

(a) if participating in the decision would be incompatible with the attorney's obligations to a client under Rule 19–301.7 (1.7); or

(b) where the decision could have a material adverse effect on the representation of a client of the organization whose interests are adverse to a client of the attorney.

COMMENT

[1] Attorneys should be encouraged to support and participate in legal service organizations. An attorney who is an officer or a member of such an organization does not thereby have a client-attorney relationship with persons served by the organization. However, there is potential conflict between the interests of such persons and the interests of the attorney's clients. If the possibility of such conflict disqualified an attorney from serving on the board of a legal services organization, the profession's involvement in such organizations would be severely curtailed.

[2] It may be necessary in appropriate cases to reassure a client of the organization that the representation will not be affected by conflicting loyalties of a member of the board. Established, written policies in this respect can enhance the credibility of such assurances.

♦ ♦ ♦

Model Rules Comparison: Given that the Ethics 2000 Amendments to the ABA Model Rules of Professional Conduct made no changes to this Rule, Rule 19–306.3 (6.3) has not been amended and remains substantially similar to Model Rule 6.3.

RULE 6.4

LAW REFORM ACTIVITIES AFFECTING CLIENT INTERESTS

An attorney may serve as a director, officer or member of an organization involved in reform of the law or its administration notwithstanding that the reform may affect the interests of a client of the attorney. When the attorney knows that the interests of a client may be materially benefitted by a decision in which the attorney participates, the attorney shall disclose that fact but need not identify the client.

COMMENT

[1] Attorneys involved in organizations seeking law reform generally do not have a client-attorney relationship with the organization. Otherwise, it might follow that an attorney could not be involved in a bar association law reform program that might indirectly affect a client. See also Rule 19–301.2 (b) (1.2). For example, an attorney specializing in antitrust litigation might be regarded as disqualified from participating in drafting revisions of rules governing that subject. In determining the nature and scope of participation in such activities, an attorney should be mindful of obligations to clients under other Rules, particularly Rule 19–301.7 (1.7). An attorney is professionally obligated to protect the integrity of the program by making an appropriate disclosure within the organization when the attorney knows a private client might be materially benefitted.

♦ ♦ ♦

Model Rules Comparison: Given that the Ethics 2000 Amendments to the ABA Model Rules of Professional Conduct made no changes to this Rule, Rule 19–306.4 (6.4) has not been amended and remains substantially similar to Model Rule 6.4.

RULE 6.5

NONPROFIT AND COURT-ANNEXED LIMITED LEGAL SERVICES PROGRAMS

(a) An attorney who, under the auspices of a program sponsored by a nonprofit organization or court, provides short-term limited legal services to a client without expectation by either the attorney or the client that the attorney will provide continuing representation in the matter:

(1) is subject to Rules 19–301.7 (1.7) and 19–301.9 (a) (1.9) only if the attorney knows that the representation of the client involves a conflict of interest; and

(2) is subject to Rule 19–301.10 (1.10) only if the attorney knows that another attorney associated with the attorney in a law firm is disqualified by Rule 19–301.7 (1.7) or 19–301.9 (a) (1.9) with respect to the matter.

(b) Except as provided in subsection (a)(2) of this Rule, Rule 19–301.10 (1.10) is inapplicable to a representation governed by this Rule.

COMMENT

[1] Legal services organizations, courts and various nonprofit organizations have established programs through which attorneys provide short-term limited legal services—such as advice or the completion of legal forms—that will assist persons to address their legal problems without further representation by an attorney. In these programs, such as legal-advice hotlines, advice-only clinics, self-represented counseling programs, or programs in which attorneys represent clients on a pro bono basis for the purposes of mediation only, a client-attorney relationship is established, but there is no expectation that the

attorney's representation of the client will continue beyond the limited consultation.

[2] An attorney who provides short-term limited legal services pursuant to this Rule must secure the client's informed consent to the limited scope of the representation. See Rule 19–301.2 (c) (1.2). If a short-term limited representation would not be reasonable under the circumstances, the attorney may offer advice to the client but must also advise the client of the need for further assistance of an attorney. Except as provided in this Rule, the Maryland Attorneys' Rules of Professional Conduct, including Rules 19–301.6 (1.6) and 19–301.9 (c) (1.9), are applicable to the limited representation.

[3] Because the limited nature of the services significantly reduces the risk of conflicts of interest with other matters being handled by the attorney's firm, section (b) provides that Rule 19–301.10 (1.10) is inapplicable to a representation governed by this Rule except as provided by subsection (a)(2) of this Rule. Subsection (a)(2) of this Rule requires the participating attorney to comply with Rule 19–301.10 (1.10) when the attorney knows that the attorney's firm is disqualified by Rules 19–301.7 (1.7) or 19–301.9 (a) (1.9). By virtue of section (b) of this Rule, however, an attorney's participation in a short-term limited legal services program will not preclude the attorney's firm from undertaking or continuing the representation of a client with interests adverse to a client being represented under the program's auspices. Nor will the personal disqualification of an attorney participating in the program be imputed to other attorneys participating in the program.

[4] If, after commencing a short-term limited representation in accordance with this Rule, an attorney undertakes to represent the client in the matter on an ongoing basis, Rules 19–301.7 (1.7), 19–301.9 (a) (1.9) and 19–301.10 (1.10) become applicable.

♦ ♦ ♦

Model Rules Comparison: This Rule, newly added to the Model Rules by the Ethics 2000 Amendments to the ABA Model Rules of Professional Conduct, is substantially similar to the ABA Rule, with the exception of changes to Comment [1] and the omission of ABA Comment [3].

INFORMATION ABOUT LEGAL SERVICES

RULE 7.1

COMMUNICATIONS CONCERNING A LAWYER'S SERVICES

An attorney shall not make a false or misleading communication about the attorney or the attorney's services. A communication is false or misleading if it:

(a) contains a material misrepresentation of fact or law, or omits a fact necessary to make the statement considered as a whole not materially misleading;

(b) is likely to create an unjustified expectation about results the attorney can achieve, or states or implies that the attorney can achieve results by means that violate the Maryland Attorneys' Rules of Professional Conduct or other law; or

(c) compares the attorney's services with other attorneys' services, unless the comparison can be factually substantiated.

COMMENT

[1] This Rule governs all communications about an attorney's services, including advertising and direct personal contact with potential clients permitted by Rules 19–307.2 (7.2) and 19–307.3 (7.3). Whatever means are used to make known an attorney's services, statements about them should be truthful. The prohibition in section (b) of this Rule of statements that may create "unjustified expectations" would ordinarily preclude advertisements about results obtained on behalf of a client, such as the amount of a damage award or the attorney's record in obtaining favorable verdicts, and advertisements containing client endorsements. Such information may create the unjustified expectation that similar results can be obtained for others without reference to the specific factual and legal circumstances.

[2] A communication will be regarded as false or misleading if it (1) asserts the attorney's record in obtaining favorable awards, verdicts, judgments, or settlements in prior cases, unless it also expressly and conspicuously states that each case is different and

that the past record is no assurance that the attorney will be successful in reaching a favorable result in any future case, or (2) contains an endorsement or testimonial as to the attorney's legal services or abilities by a person who is not a bona fide pre- existing client of the attorney and has not in fact benefitted as such from those services or abilities.

[3] See also Rule 19–308.4 (f) (8.4) for the prohibition against stating or implying an ability to influence a government agency or official or to achieve results by means that violate the Maryland Attorneys' Rules of Professional Conduct or other law.

♦ ♦ ♦

Model Rules Comparison: This Rule substantially retains existing Maryland language and does not adopt Ethics 2000 Amendments to the ABA Model Rules of Professional Conduct.

RULE 7.2

ADVERTISING

(a) Subject to the requirements of Rules 19–307.1 (7.1) and 19–307.3 (b) (7.3), an attorney may advertise services through public media, such as a telephone directory, legal directory, newspaper or other periodical, outdoor, radio or television advertising, or through communications not involving in person contact.

(b) A copy or recording of an advertisement or such other communication shall be kept for at least three years after its last dissemination along with a record of when and where it was used.

(c) An attorney shall not give anything of value to a person for recommending the attorney's services, except that an attorney may:

(1) pay the reasonable cost of advertising or written communication permitted by this Rule;

(2) pay the usual charges of a legal service plan or a not-for-profit attorney referral service;

(3) pay for a law practice purchased in accordance with Rule 19–301.17 (1.17); and

(4) refer clients to a non-attorney professional pursuant to an agreement not otherwise prohibited under these Rules that

provides for the non-attorney professional to refer clients or customers to the attorney, if:

(A) the reciprocal agreement is not exclusive, and

(B) the client is informed of the existence and nature of the agreement.

(d) Any communication made pursuant to this Rule shall include the name of at least one attorney responsible for its content.

(e) An advertisement or communication indicating that no fee will be charged in the absence of a recovery shall also disclose whether the client will be liable for any expenses.

♦ ♦ ♦

Cross reference: Maryland Attorneys' Rules of Professional Conduct, Rule 19–301.8 (e) (1.8).

♦ ♦ ♦

(f) An attorney, including a participant in an advertising group or lawyer referral service or other program involving communications concerning the attorney's services, shall be personally responsible for compliance with the provisions of Rules 19–307.1 (7.1), 19–307.2 (7.2), 19–307.3 (7.3), 19–307.4 (7.4), and 19–307.5 (7.5) and shall be prepared to substantiate such compliance.

COMMENT

[1] To assist the public in obtaining legal services, attorneys should be allowed to make known their services not only through reputation but also through organized information campaigns in the form of advertising. Advertising involves an active quest for clients, contrary to the tradition that an attorney should not seek clientele. However, the public's need to know about legal services can be fulfilled in part through advertising. This need is particularly acute in the case of persons of moderate means who have not made extensive use of legal services. The interest in expanding public information about legal services ought to prevail over considerations of tradition. Nevertheless, advertising by attorneys entails the risk of practices that are misleading or over-reaching.

[2] This Rule permits public dissemination of information concerning an attorney's name or firm name, address and telephone number; the kinds of services the attorney will undertake; the basis on which the attorney's fees are determined, including prices for specific services and payment and credit arrangements; an attorney's foreign language ability; names of references and, with their consent, names of clients regularly represented; and other information that might invite the attention of those seeking legal assistance.

[3] Questions of effectiveness and taste in advertising are matters of speculation and subjective judgment. Some jurisdictions have had extensive prohibitions against television advertising, against advertising going beyond specified facts about an attorney, or against "undignified" advertising. Television is now one of the most powerful media for getting information to the public, particularly persons of low and moderate income; prohibiting television advertising, therefore, would impede the flow of information about legal services to many sectors of the public. Limiting the information that may be advertised has a similar effect and assumes that the bar can accurately forecast the kind of information that the public would regard as relevant.

[4] Neither this Rule nor Rule 19–307.3 (7.3) prohibits communications authorized by law, such as notice to members of a class in class action litigation.

[5] Section (a) of this Rule permits communication by mail to a specific individual as well as general mailings, but does not permit contact by telephone or in person delivery of written material except through the postal service or other delivery service.

Record of Advertising

[6] Section (b) of this Rule requires that a record of the content and use of advertising be kept in order to facilitate enforcement of this Rule. It does not require that advertising be subject to review prior to dissemination. Such a requirement would be burdensome and expensive relative to its possible benefits, and may be of doubtful constitutionality.

Paying Others to Recommend an Attorney

[7] An attorney is allowed to pay for advertising permitted by this Rule and for the purchase of a law practice in accordance with the provisions of Rule 19–301.17 (1.17), but otherwise is not permitted to pay another person for channeling professional work. This restriction does not prevent an organization or person other than the attorney from advertising or recommending the attorney's services. Thus, a legal aid agency or prepaid legal services plan may pay to advertise legal services provided under its auspices. Likewise, an attorney may participate in not-for-profit attorney referral programs and pay the usual fees charged by such programs. Section (c) of this Rule does not prohibit paying regular compensation to an assistant, such as a secretary, to prepare communications permitted by this Rule.

Assignments or Referrals from a Legal Services Plan or Attorney Referral Service

[8] An attorney who accepts assignments or referrals from a legal services plan or referrals from a attorney referral service must act reasonably to assure that the activities of the plan or service are compatible with the attorney's professional obligations. See Rule 19–305.3 (5.3). Legal service plans and attorney referral services may communicate with prospective clients, but such communications must be in conformity with these Rules. Thus, advertising must not be false or misleading, as would be the case if the communications of a group advertising program or a group legal services plan would mislead prospective clients to think that it was attorney referral service sponsored by a state agency or bar association. Nor could the attorney allow in-person, telephonic, or real-time contacts that would violate Rule 19–307.3 (7.3).

Reciprocal Referral Agreements with Non-attorney Professionals

[9] An attorney may agree to refer clients to a non-attorney professional, in return for the undertaking of that person to refer clients or customers to the attorney to provide them with legal services. Such reciprocal referral arrangements must not be exclusive or otherwise interfere

with the attorney's professional judgment as to making referrals or as to providing substantive legal services. See Rules 19–302.1 (2.1) and 19–305.4 (c) (5.4). The client must also be informed of the existence and nature of the referral agreement. Reciprocal referral agreements should not be of indefinite duration and should be reviewed periodically to determine whether they comply with these Rules. Conflicts of interest created by such arrangements are governed by Rule 19–301.7 (1.7). Referral agreements between attorneys who are not in the same firm are governed by Rule 19–301.5 (e) (1.5).

Responsibility for Compliance

[10] Every attorney who participates in communications concerning the attorney's services is responsible for assuring that the specified Rules are complied with and must be prepared to substantiate compliance with those Rules. That may require retaining records for more than the three years specified in section (b) of this Rule.

♦ ♦ ♦

Model Rules Comparison: This Rule substantially retains existing Maryland language and does not adopt Ethics 2000 Amendments to the ABA Model Rules of Professional Conduct, with the exception of: (1) adding in substantial part ABA Rule 7.2 (c)(4) as adopted by the ABA House of Delegates on August 13, 2002; (2) adding ABA Comment [7] (Comment [8] above); (3) adding ABA Comment [8] (Comment [9] above).

RULE 7.3

DIRECT CONTACT WITH PROSPECTIVE CLIENTS

(a) An attorney shall not by in-person, live telephone or real-time electronic contact solicit professional employment from a prospective client when a significant motive for the attorney's doing so is the attorney's pecuniary gain, unless the person contacted:

(1) is an attorney; or

(2) has a family, close personal, or prior professional relationship with the attorney.

(b) An attorney shall not solicit professional employment from a prospective client by written, recorded or electronic communication or by in-person, telephone, or real-time electronic contact even when not otherwise prohibited by section (a), if:

(1) the attorney knows or reasonably should know that the physical, emotional or mental state of the prospective client is such that the prospective client could not exercise reasonable judgment in employing an attorney;

(2) the prospective client has made known to the attorney a desire not to be solicited by the attorney; or

(3) the solicitation involves coercion, duress, or harassment.

(c) Every written, recorded, or electronic communication from an attorney soliciting professional employment from a prospective client known to be in need of legal services in a particular matter shall include the words "Advertising Material" on the outside envelope, if any, and at the beginning and ending of any recorded or electronic communication, unless the recipient of the communication is a person specified in subsections (a)(1) or (a)(2) of this Rule.

(d) Notwithstanding the prohibitions in section (a) of this Rule, an attorney may participate with a prepaid or group legal service plan operated by an organization not owned or directed by the attorney that uses in-person or telephone contact to solicit memberships or subscriptions for the plan from persons who are not known to need legal services in a particular matter covered by the plan.

♦ ♦ ♦

Cross reference: For additional restrictions and requirements for certain communications, see Md. Code, Business Occupations and Professions Article, §§ 10–605.1 and 10–605.2.

COMMENT

[1] There is a potential for abuse inherent in direct in-person, live telephone or real-time electronic contact by an attorney with a prospective client known to need legal services. These forms of contact between an attorney and a prospective client subject the layperson to the private importuning of the trained advocate in a direct interpersonal encounter. The prospective client, who may already feel overwhelmed by the circumstances giving rise to the need for legal

services, may find it difficult fully to evaluate all available alternatives with reasoned judgment and appropriate self-interest in the face of the attorney's presence and insistence upon being retained immediately. The situation is fraught with the possibility of undue influence, intimidation, and over-reaching.

[2] This potential for abuse inherent in direct in-person, live telephone or real-time electronic solicitation of prospective clients justifies its prohibition, particularly since attorney advertising and written and recorded communication permitted under Rule 19–307.2 (7.2) offer alternative means of conveying necessary information to those who may be in need of legal services. Advertising and written and recorded communications which may be mailed or autodialed make it possible for a prospective client to be informed about the need for legal services, and about the qualifications of available attorneys and law firms, without subjecting the prospective client to direct in-person, telephone or real-time electronic persuasion that may overwhelm the client's judgment.

[3] The use of general advertising and written, recorded or electronic communications to transmit information from attorney to prospective client, rather than direct in-person, live telephone or real-time electronic contact, will help to assure that the information flows cleanly as well as freely. The contents of advertisements and communications permitted under Rule 19–307.2 (7.2) can be permanently recorded so that they cannot be disputed and may be shared with others who know the attorney. This potential for informal review is itself likely to help guard against statements and claims that might constitute false and misleading communications, in violation of Rule 19–307.1 (7.1). The contents of direct in-person, live telephone or real-time electronic conversations between an attorney and a prospective client can be disputed and may not be subject to third-party scrutiny. Consequently, they are much more likely to approach (and occasionally cross) the dividing line between accurate representations and those that are false and misleading.

[4] There is far less likelihood that an attorney would engage in abusive practices against a person who is a former client, or with whom the attorney has a close personal or family relationship, or

in situations in which the attorney is motivated by considerations other than the attorney's pecuniary gain. Nor is there a serious potential for abuse when the person contacted is an attorney. Consequently, the general prohibition in Rule 19–307.3 (a) (7.3) and the requirements of Rule 19–307.3 (c) (7.3) are not applicable in those situations. Also, section (a) is not intended to prohibit an attorney from participating in constitutionally protected activities of public or charitable legal-service organizations or bona fide political, social, civic, fraternal, employee or trade organizations whose purposes include providing or recommending legal services to its members or beneficiaries.

[5] But even permitted forms of solicitation can be abused. Thus, any solicitation which contains information which is false or misleading within the meaning of Rule 19–307.1 (7.1), which involves coercion, duress or harassment within the meaning of Rule 19–307.3 (b)(2) (7.3), or which involves contact with a prospective client who has made known to the attorney a desire not to be solicited by the attorney within the meaning of Rule 19–307.3 (b)(2) (7.3) is prohibited. Moreover, if after sending a letter or other communication to a client as permitted by Rule 19–307.2 (7.2) the attorney receives no response, any further effort to communicate with the prospective client may violate the provisions of Rule 19–307.3 (b) (7.3).

[6] This Rule is not intended to prohibit an attorney from contacting representatives of organizations or groups that may be interested in establishing a group or prepaid legal plan for their members, insureds, beneficiaries or other third parties for the purpose of informing such entities of the availability of and details concerning the plan or arrangement which the attorney or attorney's firm is willing to offer. This form of communication is not directed to a prospective client. Rather, it is usually addressed to an individual acting in a fiduciary capacity seeking a supplier of legal services for others who may, if they choose, become prospective clients of the attorney. Under these circumstances, the activity which the attorney undertakes in communicating with such representatives and the type of information transmitted to the individual are functionally similar

to and serve the same purpose as advertising permitted under Rule 19–307.2 (7.2).

[7] The requirement in Rule 19–307.3 (c) (7.3) that certain communications be marked "Advertising Material" does not apply to communications sent in response to requests of potential clients or their spokespersons or sponsors. General announcements by attorneys, including changes in personnel or office location, do not constitute communications soliciting professional employment from a client known to be in need of legal services within the meaning of this Rule.

[8] Section (d) of this Rule permits an attorney to participate with an organization that uses personal contact to solicit members for its group or prepaid legal service plan, provided that the personal contact is not undertaken by any attorney who would be a provider of legal services through the plan. The organization must not be owned by or directed (whether as manager or otherwise) by any attorney or law firm that participates in the plan. For example, section (d) of this Rule would not permit an attorney to create an organization controlled directly or indirectly by the attorney and use the organization for the in-person or telephone solicitation of legal employment of the attorney through memberships in the plan or otherwise. The communication permitted by these organizations also must not be directed to a person known to need legal services in a particular matter, but is to be designed to inform potential plan members generally of another means of affordable legal services. Attorneys who participate in a legal service plan must reasonably assure that the plan sponsors are in compliance with Rules 19–307.1 (7.1), 19–307.2 (7.2) and 19–307.3 (b) (7.3). See 19–308.4 (a) (8.4).

♦ ♦ ♦

Model Rules Comparison: Rule 19–307.3 (7.3) is substantially similar to the language of the Ethics 2000 Amendments to the ABA Model Rules of Professional Conduct, with the exception of retaining existing Maryland language in 19–307.3 (b)(1) (7.3) and accordingly redesignating the subsections of Rule 19–307.3 (b) (7.3).

RULE 7.4

COMMUNICATION OF FIELDS OF PRACTICE

(a) An attorney may communicate the fact that the attorney does or does not practice in particular fields of law, subject to the requirements of Rule 19–307.1 (7.1).

(b) An attorney admitted to engage in patent practice before the United States Patent and Trademark Office may use the designation "Patent Attorney" or a substantially similar designation.

COMMENT

[1] This Rule permits an attorney to indicate areas of practice in communications about the attorney's services; for example, in a telephone directory or other advertising. If attorney practices only in such fields, or will not accept matters except in such fields, the attorney is permitted so to indicate.

[2] Section (b) of this Rule recognizes the long-established policy of the Patent and Trademark Office for the designation of attorneys practicing before the Office.

♦ ♦ ♦

Model Rules Comparison—This Rule adopts Rule 7.4 (a) and (b) of the ABA Model Rules of Professional Conduct, and expressly makes section (a) "subject to the requirement of Rule 19–307.1 (7.1)." The substance of the first two sentences of the ABA Comment on Rule 7.4 (a) is included in Comment [1], and the ABA Comment on Rule 7.4 (b) is included as Comment [2].

RULE 7.5

FIRM NAMES AND LETTERHEADS

(a) An attorney shall not use a firm name, letterhead or other professional designation that violates Rule 19–307.1 (7.1). A trade name may be used by an attorney in private practice if it does not imply a connection with a government agency or with a public or charitable legal services organization and is not otherwise in violation of Rule 19–307.1 (7.1).

(b) A law firm with offices in more than one jurisdiction may use the same name in each jurisdiction, but identification of the attorneys in an office of the firm shall indicate the jurisdictional limitations on those not licensed to practice in the jurisdiction where the office is located.

(c) The name of an attorney holding a public office shall not be used in the name of a law firm, or in communications on its behalf, during any substantial period in which the attorney is not actively and regularly practicing with the firm.

(d) Attorneys may state or imply that they practice in a partnership or other organization only when that is the fact.

COMMENT

[1] A firm may be designated by the names of all or some of its members, by the names of deceased or retired members where there has been a continuing succession in the firm's identity or by a trade name such as the "ABC Legal Clinic." A firm may not be designated by the names of non-attorneys. See Rule 19–305.4 (5.4). Although the United States Supreme Court has held that legislation may prohibit the use of trade names in professional practice, use of such names in law practice is acceptable so long as it is not misleading. It may be observed that any firm name including the name of a deceased partner is, strictly speaking, a trade name. The use of such names to designate law firms has proven a useful means of identification. However, it is misleading to use the name of an attorney not associated with the firm or a predecessor of the firm, or the name of a non-attorney.

[2] An attorney in private practice may not practice under a name which implies any connection with the government or any agency of the federal government, any state or any political subdivision, or with a public or charitable legal services organization. This is to prevent a situation where non-attorneys might conclude that they are dealing with an agency established or sanctioned by the government, or one funded by either the government or public

contributions and thus charging lower fees. The use of any of the following ordinarily would violate this Rule:

(1) The proper name of a government unit, whether or not identified with the type of unit. Thus, a name could be the basis of a disciplinary proceeding if it included the designation "Annapolis" or "City of Annapolis," "Baltimore," or "Baltimore County," "Maryland," or "Maryland State" (which could be a violation as a confusing although mistaken reference to the state or under Comment [3]).

(2) The generic name of any form of government unit found in the same area where the firm practices, e.g. national, state, county, or municipal.

(3) The name of or a reference to a college, university, or other institution of higher learning, regardless of whether it has a law school, unless the provider of legal higher learning. For example, the names "Georgetown Legal Clinic (or "Law Office," etc.)" and "U.B. Legal Clinic (or "Law Office," etc.)" could both violate this Rule if used by unaffiliated organizations.

(4) The words "public," "government," "civic," "legal aid," "community," "neighborhood," or other words of similar import suggesting that the legal services offered are at least in part publicly funded. Although names such as "Neighborhood Legal Clinic of John Doe" might otherwise appear unobjectionable, the terms "legal aid," "community" and "neighborhood" have become so associated with public or charitable legal services organizations as to form the basis of disciplinary proceedings.

[3] Firm names which include geographical names which are not also government units, or adjectives merely suggesting the context of the practice (e.g., "urban," "rural") ordinarily would not violate Rule 19–307.5 (7.5). The acceptability of the use of a proper or generic name of a government unit when coupled with an adjective or further description (beyond mere reference to the provision of legal services) should be judged by the general policy underlying Rule 19–307.5 (7.5), and any doubt regarding the misleading connotations of a name may be resolved against use of the name.

[4] With regard to section (d) of this Rule, attorneys sharing office facilities, but who are not in fact partners, may not denominate themselves as, for example, "Smith and Jones," for that title suggests partnership in the practice of law.

♦ ♦ ♦

Model Rules Comparison: This Rule substantially retains existing Maryland language and does not adopt Ethics 2000 Amendments to the ABA Model Rules of Professional Conduct, with the exception of changes to Comment [1].

MAINTAINING THE INTEGRITY OF THE PROFESSION

RULE 8.1

BAR ADMISSION AND DISCIPLINARY MATTERS

An applicant for admission or reinstatement to the bar, or an attorney in connection with a bar admission application or in connection with a disciplinary matter, shall not:

(a) knowingly make a false statement of material fact; or

(b) fail to disclose a fact necessary to correct a misapprehension known by the person to have arisen in the matter, or knowingly fail to respond to a lawful demand for information from an admissions or disciplinary authority, except that this Rule does not require disclosure of information otherwise protected by Rule 19–301.6 (1.6).

COMMENT

[1] The duty imposed by this Rule extends to persons seeking admission or reinstatement to the bar as well as to attorneys. Hence, if a person makes a material false statement in connection with an application for admission or for reinstatement, the statement may be the basis for subsequent disciplinary action if the person is admitted or reinstated, and in any event may be relevant in a subsequent admission application. The duty imposed by this Rule applies to an attorney's own admission or discipline as well as that of others. Thus, it is a separate professional offense for an attorney to knowingly make a misrepresentation or omission in connection

with a disciplinary investigation of the attorney's own conduct. This Rule also requires affirmative clarification of any misunderstanding on the part of the admissions or disciplinary authority of which the person involved becomes aware.

[2] The Supreme Court has considered this Rule applicable when information is sought by the Attorney Grievance Commission from any attorney on any matter, whether or not the attorney is personally involved. See *Attorney Grievance Commission v. Oswinkle*, 364 Md. 182 (2001).

[3] This Rule is subject to the provisions of the Fifth Amendment of the United States Constitution and corresponding provisions of state constitutions. A person relying on such a provision in response to a question, however, should do so openly and not use the right of nondisclosure as a justification for failure to comply with this Rule.

[4] An attorney representing an applicant for admission to the bar, or representing an attorney who is the subject of a disciplinary inquiry or proceeding, is governed by the rules applicable to the client-attorney relationship.

♦ ♦ ♦

Cross reference: Md. Rule 19–701 (s) (defining "Reinstatement").

Model Rules Comparison: This Rule substantially retains existing Maryland language with some further revisions and does not adopt Ethics 2000 Amendments to the ABA Model Rules of Professional Conduct.

RULE 8.2

JUDICIAL AND LEGAL OFFICIALS

(a) An attorney shall not make a statement that the attorney knows to be false or with reckless disregard as to its truth or falsity concerning the qualifications or integrity of a judge, adjudicatory officer or public legal officer, or of a candidate for election or appointment to judicial or legal office.

(b) Rule 18–104.1 (c)(2)(D) (4.1) of the Maryland Code of Judicial Conduct, set forth in Title 18, Chapter 100, provides that an attorney becomes a candidate for a judicial office when the attorney files a certificate of candidacy in accordance with Maryland election laws, but no earlier than two years prior to the general election for that office. A candidate for a judicial office:

(1) shall maintain the dignity appropriate to the office and act in a manner consistent with the impartiality, independence and integrity of the judiciary;

(2) with respect to a case, controversy, or issue that is likely to come before the court, shall not make a commitment, pledge, or promise that is inconsistent with the impartial performance of the adjudicative duties of the office;

♦ ♦ ♦

Committee note: Rule 19–308.2 (b)(2) (8.2) does not prohibit a candidate from making a commitment, pledge, or promise respecting improvements in court administration or the faithful and impartial performance of the duties of the office.

♦ ♦ ♦

(3) shall not knowingly misrepresent his or her identity or qualifications, the identity or qualifications of an opponent, or any other fact;

(4) shall not allow any other person to do for the candidate what the candidate is prohibited from doing; and

(5) may respond to a personal attack or an attack on the candidate's record as long as the response does not otherwise violate this Rule.

COMMENT

[1] Assessments by attorneys are relied on in evaluating the professional or personal fitness of individuals being considered for election or appointment to judicial office and to public legal offices, such as attorney general, prosecuting attorney and public defender. Expressing honest and candid opinions on such matters contributes to improving the administration of justice. Conversely, false statements by an attorney can unfairly undermine public confidence in the administration of justice.

[2] To maintain the fair and independent administration of justice, attorneys are encouraged to continue traditional efforts to defend judges and courts unjustly criticized.

♦ ♦ ♦

Model Rules Comparison: Rule 19–308.2 (8.2) revises prior Maryland language without adopting Ethics 2000 Amendments to the ABA Model Rules of Professional Conduct.

RULE 8.3

REPORTING PROFESSIONAL MISCONDUCT

(a) An attorney who knows that another attorney has committed a violation of the Maryland Attorneys' Rules of Professional Conduct that raises a substantial question as to that attorney's honesty, trustworthiness or fitness as an attorney in other respects, shall inform the appropriate professional authority.

(b) An attorney who knows that a judge has committed a violation of applicable rules of judicial conduct that raises a substantial question as to the judge's fitness for office shall inform the appropriate authority.

(c) This Rule does not require disclosure of information otherwise protected by Rule 19–301.6 (1.6) or information gained by an attorney or judge while participating in an attorney or judge assistance or professional guidance program.

COMMENT

[1] Self-regulation of the legal profession requires that members of the profession initiate disciplinary investigation when they know of a violation of the Maryland Attorneys' Rules of Professional Conduct. Attorneys have a similar obligation with respect to judicial misconduct. An apparently isolated violation may indicate a pattern of misconduct that only a disciplinary investigation can uncover. Reporting a violation is especially important where the victim is unlikely to discover the offense. For the definition of "knows" under these Rules, see Rule 19–301.0 (h) (1.0).

[2] A report about misconduct is not required where it would involve violation of Rule 19–301.6 (1.6). However, an attorney should encourage a client to consent to disclosure where prosecution would not substantially prejudice the client's interests.

[3] If an attorney were obliged to report every violation of the Rules, the failure to report any violation would itself be a professional offense. Such a requirement existed in many jurisdictions but proved to be unenforceable. This Rule limits the reporting obligation to those offenses that a self-regulating profession must vigorously endeavor to prevent. A measure of judgment is, therefore, required in complying with the provisions of this Rule. The term "substantial" refers to the seriousness of the possible offense and not the quantum of evidence of which the attorney is aware. A report should be made to the bar disciplinary agency unless some other agency, such as a peer review agency, is more appropriate in the circumstances. Similar considerations apply to the reporting of judicial misconduct.

[4] The duty to report professional misconduct does not apply to an attorney retained to represent an attorney whose professional conduct is in question. Such a situation is governed by the rules applicable to the client-attorney relationship.

[5] Information about an attorney's or judge's misconduct or fitness may be received by an attorney in the course of that attorney's participation in an approved attorney or judge assistance or professional guidance program. In that circumstance, providing for an exception to the reporting requirements of sections (a) and (b) of this Rule encourages attorneys and judges to seek assistance through such a program. Conversely, without such an exception, attorneys and judges may hesitate to seek assistance from these programs, which may then result in harm to their professional careers and injury to the welfare of client and the public. These Rules do not otherwise address the confidentiality of information received by an attorney or judge participating in such programs; such an obligation, however, may be imposed by the rules of the program or other law.

♦ ♦ ♦

Model Rules Comparison: Rule 19–308.3 (8.3) is substantially similar to the Ethics 2000 Amendments to the ABA Model Rules of Professional Conduct, with the exception of wording changes to Rule 19–308.3 (c) (8.3) and Comment [5].

RULE 8.4

MISCONDUCT

It is professional misconduct for an attorney to:

(a) violate or attempt to violate the Maryland Attorneys' Rules of Professional Conduct, knowingly assist or induce another to do so, or do so through the acts of another;

(b) commit a criminal act that reflects adversely on the attorney's honesty, trustworthiness or fitness as an attorney in other respects;

(c) engage in conduct involving dishonesty, fraud, deceit or misrepresentation;

(d) engage in conduct that is prejudicial to the administration of justice;

(e) knowingly manifest by words or conduct when acting in a professional capacity bias or prejudice based upon race, sex, religion, national origin, disability, age, sexual orientation or socioeconomic status when such action is prejudicial to the administration of justice, provided, however, that legitimate advocacy is not a violation of this section;

(f) state or imply an ability to influence improperly a government agency or official or to achieve results by means that violate the Maryland Attorneys' Rules of Professional Conduct or other law; or

(g) knowingly assist a judge or judicial officer in conduct that is a violation of applicable rules of judicial conduct or other law.

COMMENT

[1] Attorneys are subject to discipline when they violate or attempt to violate the Maryland Attorneys' Rules of Professional Conduct, knowingly assist or induce another to do so or do so through the acts of another, as when they request or instruct an agent to do so on the attorney's behalf. Section (a) of this Rule, however, does not prohibit an attorney from advising a client concerning action the client is legally entitled to take.

[2] Many kinds of illegal conduct reflect adversely on fitness to practice law, such as offenses involving fraud and the offense of willful failure to file an income tax return. However, some kinds of

offense carry no such implication. Traditionally, the distinction was drawn in terms of offenses involving "moral turpitude." That concept can be construed to include offenses concerning some matters of personal morality, such as adultery and comparable offenses, that have no specific connection to fitness for the practice of law. Although an attorney is personally answerable to the entire criminal law, attorney should be professionally answerable only for offenses that indicate lack of those characteristics relevant to law practice. Offenses involving violence, dishonesty, or breach of trust, or serious interference with the administration of justice are in that category. A pattern of repeated offenses, even ones of minor significance when considered separately, can indicate indifference to legal obligation.

[3] Sexual misconduct or sexual harassment involving colleagues, clients, or co-workers may violate section (d) or (e) of this Rule. This could occur, for example, where coercion or undue influence is used to obtain sexual favor in exploitation of these relationships. See *Attorney Grievance Commission v. Goldsborough*, 330 Md. 342 (1993). See also Rule 19–301.7 (1.7).

[4] Section (e) of this Rule reflects the premise that a commitment to equal justice under the law lies at the very heart of the legal system. As a result, even when not otherwise unlawful, an attorney who, while acting in a professional capacity, engages in the conduct described in section (e) of this Rule and by so doing prejudices the administration of justice commits a particularly egregious type of discrimination. Such conduct manifests a lack of character required of members of the legal profession. A trial judge's finding that peremptory challenges were exercised on a discriminatory basis does not alone establish a violation of this rule. A judge, however, must require attorneys to refrain from the conduct described in section (e) of this Rule. See Md. Rule 18–102.3.

[5] An attorney may refuse to comply with an obligation imposed by law upon a good faith belief that no valid obligation exists. The provisions of Rule 19–301.2 (d) (1.2) concerning a good faith challenge to the validity, scope, meaning or application of the law apply to challenges to legal regulation of the practice of law.

[6] Attorneys holding public office assume legal responsibilities going beyond those of other citizens. A attorney's abuse of public office can suggest an inability to fulfill the professional role of attorney. The same is true of abuse of positions of private trust such as trustee, executor, administrator, guardian, agent and officer, director or manager of a corporation or other organization.

♦ ♦ ♦

Model Rules Comparison: Rule 19–308.4 (8.4) is substantially similar to the language of the Ethics 2000 Amendments to the ABA Model Rules of Professional Conduct, with the exception of adding Rule 19–308.4 (e) (8.4) and redesignating the subsections of Rule 19–308.4 (8.4) as appropriate, adding Comment [4] above, and retaining Comment [3] above from existing Maryland language.

RULE 8.5

Disciplinary Authority; Choice of Law

(a) Disciplinary Authority.

(1) An attorney admitted by the Supreme Court to practice in this State is subject to the disciplinary authority of this State, regardless of where the attorney's conduct occurs.

(2) An attorney not admitted to practice in this State is also subject to the disciplinary authority of this State if the attorney:

(A) provides or offers to provide any legal services in this State,

(B) holds himself or herself out as practicing law in this State, or

(C) has an obligation to supervise or control another attorney practicing law in this State whose conduct constitutes a violation of these Rules.

♦ ♦ ♦

Cross reference: Md. Rule 19–701 (b).

♦ ♦ ♦

(3) An attorney may be subject to the disciplinary authority of both this State and another jurisdiction for the same conduct.

(b) **Choice of Law.** In any exercise of the disciplinary authority of this State, the rule of professional conduct to be applied shall be as follows:

(1) for conduct in connection with a matter pending before a tribunal, the rules of the jurisdiction in which the tribunal sits, unless the rules of the tribunal provide otherwise; and

(2) for any other conduct, the rules of the jurisdiction in which the attorney's conduct occurred, or, if the predominant effect of the conduct is in a different jurisdiction, the rules of that jurisdiction shall be applied to the conduct. An attorney shall not be subject to discipline if the attorney's conduct conforms to the rules of a jurisdiction in which the attorney reasonably believes the predominant effect of the attorney's conduct will occur.

COMMENT

Disciplinary Authority

[1] It is longstanding law that the conduct of an attorney admitted to practice in this State is subject to the disciplinary authority of this State. Extension of the disciplinary authority of this State to other attorneys who provide or offer to provide legal services in this State is for the protection of the citizens of this State. Reciprocal enforcement of a jurisdiction's disciplinary findings and sanctions will further advance the purposes of this Rule. An attorney who is subject to the disciplinary authority of this State under Rule 19–308.5 (a) (8.5) appoints an official to be designated by this Court to receive service of process in this State.

Choice of Law

[2] An attorney may be potentially subject to more than one set of rules of professional conduct that impose different obligations. The attorney may be licensed to practice in more than one jurisdiction with differing rules, or may be admitted to practice before a particular court with rules that differ from those of the jurisdiction or jurisdictions in which the attorney is licensed to practice. Additionally, the attorney's conduct may involve significant contacts with more than one jurisdiction.

[3] Section (b) of this Rule seeks to resolve such potential conflicts. Its premise is that minimizing conflicts between rules, as well as

uncertainty about which rules are applicable, is in the best interest of both clients and the profession (as well as the bodies having authority to regulate the profession). Accordingly, it takes the approach of (i) providing that any particular conduct of an attorney shall be subject to only one set of rules of professional conduct, (ii) making the determination of which set of rules applies to particular conduct as straightforward as possible, consistent with recognition of appropriate regulatory interests of relevant jurisdictions, and (iii) providing protection from discipline for attorneys who act reasonably in the face of uncertainty.

[4] Subsection (b)(1) of this Rule provides that as to an attorney's conduct relating to a proceeding pending before a tribunal, the attorney shall be subject only to the rules of professional conduct of that tribunal. As to all other conduct, including conduct in anticipation of a proceeding not yet pending before a tribunal, subsection (b)(2) of this Rule provides that an attorney shall be subject to the rules of the jurisdiction in which the attorney's conduct occurred, or, if the predominant effect of the conduct is in another jurisdiction, the rules of that jurisdiction shall be applied to the conduct. In the case of conduct in anticipation of a proceeding that is likely to be before a tribunal, the predominant effect of such conduct could be where the conduct occurred, where the tribunal sits or in another jurisdiction.

[5] When an attorney's conduct involves significant contacts with more than one jurisdiction, it may not be clear whether the predominant effect of the attorney's conduct will occur in a jurisdiction other than the one in which the conduct occurred. So long as the attorney's conduct conforms to the rules of a jurisdiction in which the attorney reasonably believes the predominant effect will occur, the attorney shall not be subject to discipline under this Rule.

[6] If two admitting jurisdictions were to proceed against attorney for the same conduct, they should, applying this Rule, identify the same governing ethics rules. They should take all appropriate steps to see that they do apply the same rule to the same conduct, and in all events should avoid proceeding against an attorney on the basis of two inconsistent rules.

[7] The choice of law provision applies to attorneys engaged in transnational practice, unless international law, treaties or other agreements between competent regulatory authorities in the affected jurisdiction provide otherwise.

♦ ♦ ♦

Model Rules Comparison: Rule 19–308.5 (a) (8.5) combines the substance of former Rules 8.5 (a) and 8.5 (b). Rule 19–308.5 (b) (8.5) is substantially similar to ABA Model Rule 8.5 (b). The Comments are substantially similar to the ABA Comments with the exception of omitting the final sentence of ABA Comment [1].

IDEALS OF PROFESSIONALISM

Professionalism is the combination of the core values of personal integrity, competency, civility, independence, and public service that distinguish attorneys as the caretakers of the rule of law.

These Ideals of Professionalism emanate from and complement the Maryland Attorneys' Rules of Professional Conduct ("MARPC"), the overall thrust of which is well-summarized in this passage from the Preamble to those Rules:

> "An attorney should use the law's procedures only for legitimate purposes and not to harass or intimidate others. An attorney should demonstrate respect for the legal system and for those who serve it, including judges, other attorneys, and public officials."

A failure to observe these Ideals is not of itself a basis for disciplinary sanctions, but the conduct that constitutes the failure may be a basis for disciplinary sanctions if it violates a provision of the MARPC or other relevant law.

Preamble

Attorneys are entrusted with the privilege of practicing law. They take a firm vow or oath to uphold the Constitution and laws of the United States and the State of Maryland. Attorneys enjoy a distinct position of trust and confidence that carries the significant responsibility and obligation to be caretakers for the system of justice that is essential to the continuing existence of a civilized society. Each attorney, therefore, as a custodian of the system of justice, must be conscious of this responsibility and exhibit traits that reflect a personal responsibility to recognize, honor, and enhance the rule of law in this society. The Ideals and some characteristics set forth below are representative of a value system that attorneys must demand of themselves as professionals in order to maintain and enhance the role of legal professionals as the protectors of the rule of law.

Ideals of Professionalism

An attorney should aspire:

(1) to put fidelity to clients before self-interest;

(2) to be a model for others, and particularly for his or her clients, by showing respect due to those called upon to resolve disputes and the regard due to all participants in the dispute resolution processes;

(3) to avoid all forms of wrongful discrimination in all of his or her activities, including discrimination on the basis of race, sex, gender, religion, national origin, ethnicity, disability, age, sexual orientation, marital status, socioeconomic status, or political affiliation, with equality and fairness as the goals;

(4) to preserve and improve the law, the legal system, and other dispute resolution processes as instruments for the common good;

(5) to make the law, the legal system, and other dispute resolution processes available to all;

(6) to practice law with a personal commitment to the rules governing the profession and to encourage others to do the same;

(7) to preserve the dignity and the integrity of the profession by his or her conduct, because the dignity and the integrity of the profession are an inheritance that must be maintained by each successive generation of attorneys;

(8) to strive for excellence in the practice of law to promote the interests of his or her clients, the rule of law, and the welfare of society; and

(9) to recognize that the practice of law is a calling in the spirit of public service, not merely a business pursuit.

Accountability and Trustworthiness

An attorney should understand the principles set forth in this section.

(1) Punctuality promotes the credibility of an attorney. Tardiness and neglect denigrate the individual, as well as the legal profession.

(2) Personal integrity is essential to the honorable practice of law. Attorneys earn the respect of clients, opposing attorneys, and the courts when they keep their commitments and perform the tasks promised.

(3) Honesty and, subject to legitimate requirements of confidentiality, candid communications promote credibility with clients, opposing attorneys, and the courts.

(4) Monetary pressures that cloud professional judgment and should be resisted.

Education, Mentoring, and Excellence

An attorney should:

(1) make constant efforts to expand his or her legal knowledge and to ensure familiarity with changes in the law that affect a client's interests;

(2) willingly take on the responsibility of promoting the image of the legal profession by educating each client and the public regarding the principles underlying the justice system, and, as a practitioner of a learned art, by conveying to everyone the importance of professionalism;

(3) attend continuing legal education programs to demonstrate a commitment to keeping abreast of changes in the law;

(4) as a senior attorney, accept the role of mentor and teacher, whether through formal education programs or individual mentoring of less experienced attorneys; and

(5) understand that mentoring includes the responsibility for setting a good example for another attorney, as well as an obligation to ensure that each mentee learns the principles enunciated in these Ideals and adheres to them in practice.

A Calling to Service

An attorney should:

(1) serve the public interest by communicating clearly with clients, opposing attorneys, judges, and the general public;

(2) consider the impact on others when scheduling events. Reasonable requests for schedule changes should be accommodated if, in the view of the attorney, such requests do not impact adversely the merits of the client's position;

(3) maintain an open and respectful dialogue with clients and opposing attorneys;

(4) respond to all communications promptly, even if more time is needed to formulate a complete answer, and understand that delays in returning telephone calls or answering mail may leave the impression that the communication was unimportant or that the message was lost, and such delays increase tension and frustration;

(5) keep a client apprised of the status of important matters affecting the client and inform the client of the frequency with which information will be provided, understanding that some matters will require regular contact, while others will require only occasional communication;

(6) always explain a client's options or choices in sufficient detail to help the client make an informed decision;

(7) reflect a spirit of respect in all interactions with opposing attorneys, parties, staff, and the court; and

(8) accept responsibility for ensuring that justice is available to every person and not just those with financial means.

Fairness, Civility, and Courtesy

An attorney should:

(1) act fairly in all dealings as a way of promoting the system of justice;

(2) understand that an excess of zeal may undermine a client's cause and hamper the administration of justice and that an attorney can advocate zealously a client's cause in a manner that remains fair and civil;

(3) know that zeal requires only that the client's interests are paramount and therefore warrant use of negotiation and compromise, when appropriate, to achieve a beneficial outcome, understanding that yelling, intimidating, issuing ultimatums, and using an "all or nothing" approach may constitute bullying, not zealous advocacy;

(4) seek to remain objective when advising a client about the strengths and weaknesses of the client's case or work;

(5) not allow a client's improper motives, unethical directions, or ill-advised wishes to influence an attorney's actions or advice, such as when deciding whether to consent to an extension of time requested by an opponent, and make that choice based on the effect, if any, on the outcome of the client's case and not on the acrimony that may exist between the parties;

(6) when appropriate and consistent with duties to the client, negotiate in good faith in an effort to avoid litigation and, where indicated, suggest alternative dispute resolution;

(7) use litigation tools to strengthen the client's case, but avoid using litigation tactics in a manner solely to harass, intimidate, or overburden an opposing party; and

(8) note explicitly any changes made to documents submitted for review by opposing attorneys, understanding that fairness is undermined by attempts to insert or delete language without notifying the other party or the party's attorney.

An attorney should understand that:

(1) professionalism requires civility in all dealings, showing respect for differing points of view, and demonstrating empathy for others;

(2) courtesy does not reflect weakness; rather, it promotes effective advocacy by ensuring that parties have the opportunity to participate in the process without personal attacks or intimidation;

(3) maintaining decorum in every venue, especially in the courtroom, is neither a relic of the past nor a sign of weakness; it is an essential component of the legal process;

(4) professionalism is enhanced by preparing scrupulously for meetings and court appearances and by showing respect for the court, opposing attorneys, and the parties through courteous behavior and respectful attire;

(5) courtesy and respect should be demonstrated in all contexts, not just with clients and colleagues, or in the courtroom, but also with support staff and court personnel;

(6) hostility between clients should not be a ground for an attorney to show hostility or disrespect to a party, an opposing attorney, or the court;

(7) patience enables an attorney to exercise restraint in volatile situations and to defuse anger, rather than elevate the tension and animosity between parties or attorneys; and

(8) the Ideals of Professionalism are to be observed in every kind of communication, and an attorney should resist the impulse to respond uncivilly to electronic communications in the same manner as he or she would resist such impulses in other forms of communication.

GUIDELINES OF ADVOCACY FOR ATTORNEYS REPRESENTING CHILDREN IN CINA AND RELATED TPR AND ADOPTION PROCEEDINGS

STATEMENT OF THE ISSUE

The Maryland Foster Care Court Improvement Project has developed these Guidelines of Advocacy for Attorneys Representing Children in Child in Need of Assistance (CINA) and Related Termination of Parental Rights (TPR) and Adoption Proceedings. The court's ability to protect the interests of children rests in large part upon the skill and expertise of the advocate. An attorney should represent a child who is the subject of a CINA or a related TPR or adoption proceeding in accordance with these Guidelines. Nothing contained in the Guidelines is intended to modify, amend, or alter the fiduciary duties that an attorney owes to a client pursuant to the Maryland Attorneys' Rules of Professional Conduct. For purposes of these Guidelines, the word "child" refers to the client of the attorney.

A. ADVOCATE FOR THE CHILD

Guideline A. Role of the Child's Counsel

The attorney should determine whether the child has considered judgment as defined in Guideline B1. If the child has considered judgment, the attorney should so state in open court and should advocate a position consistent with the child's wishes in the matter. If the attorney determines that the child lacks considered judgment, the attorney should so inform the court. The attorney should then advocate a position consistent with the best interests of the child as defined in Guideline B2.

B. CONSIDERED JUDGMENT

Guideline B1. Assessing Considered Judgment

The attorney should advocate the position of a child unless the attorney reasonably concludes that the child is unable to express a reasoned choice about issues that are relevant to the particular purpose for which the attorney is representing the child. If the child has the ability to express a reasoned choice, the child is regarded as having considered judgment.

a. To determine whether the child has considered judgment, the attorney should focus on the child's decision-making process, rather than the child's decision. The attorney should determine whether the child can understand the risks and benefits of the child's legal position and whether the child can reasonably communicate the child's wishes. The attorney should consider the following factors when determining whether the child has considered judgment:
   (1) the child's developmental stage:
      (a) cognitive ability,
      (b) socialization, and
      (c) emotional and mental development;
   (2) the child's expression of a relevant position:
      (a) ability to communicate with the attorney, and
      (b) ability to articulate reasons for the legal position; an
   (3) relevant and available reports such as reports from social workers, psychiatrists, psychologists, and schools.

b. A child may be capable of considered judgment even though the child has a significant cognitive or emotional disability.

c. At every interview with the child, the attorney should assess whether the child has considered judgment regarding each relevant issue. In making a determination regarding considered judgment, the attorney may seek guidance from professionals, family members, school officials, and other concerned persons. The attorney should also determine if any evaluations are needed and advocate them when appropriate. At no time shall the attorney compromise the attorney-client privilege.

d. An attorney should be sensitive to cultural, racial, ethnic, or economic differences between the attorney and the child because such differences may inappropriately influence the attorney's assessment of whether the child has considered judgment.

Guideline B2. Best Interest Standard

When an attorney representing a child determines that the child does not have considered judgment, the attorney should advocate for services and safety measures that the attorney believes to be in the child's best interests, taking into consideration the placement that is the least restrictive alternative. The attorney may advocate a position different from the child's wishes if the attorney finds that the child does not have considered judgment at that time. The attorney should make clear to the court that the attorney is adopting the best interest standard for that particular proceeding and state the reasons for adopting the best interest standard as well as the reasons for any change from a previously adopted standard of representation. Even if the attorney advocates a position different from the child's wishes, the attorney should ensure that the child's position is made a part of the record.

C. CLIENT CONTACT

Guideline C1. General

The attorney should meet in the community with the child at each key stage of the representation to conduct a meaningful interview. The attorney should meet the child in preparation for a hearing, regardless of the child's age or disability, in an environment that will facilitate reasonable attorney-client communications. The attorney is encouraged to meet with the child in multiple environments, including the child's school, placement, each subsequent placement, or home.

When face-to-face contact with a child is not reasonably possible or not necessary, the attorney still should have meaningful contact with the child. These situations may include: (a) a child placed out-of-state; (b) a teenager with whom the attorney has established a sufficient attorney-client relationship; or (c) a child under the age of three at the shelter care proceeding. The attorney, however, should have face-to-face contact with the child prior to the adjudication hearing.

When a communication with the child requires a sign or spoken language interpreter, the attorney should try to use the services of a court-related interpreter or other qualified interpreter other than the child's family, friends, or social workers.

Guideline C2. Determinations

After conducting one or more interviews with a child and giving reasonable consideration to the child's age and cognitive and emotional development, the attorney should determine, at a minimum:

a. whether the child has considered judgment;
b. whether the presence of the child at the proceedings will be waived, i.e., whether the child wants or needs to be present at the hearing or whether the child will be harmed by appearing in court;
c. the child's position on the agency's petition, court report(s), and other relevant issues, including the permanency plan and placement;
d. the child's position on evidence that may be offered at the hearing, including evidence that may be offered on behalf of the child;
e. the child's legal position at the hearing;
f. whether there is a conflict of interest that requires the attorney to move to withdraw from representing one or all of the clients as, for example, when the attorney represents siblings;
g. whether the child should be called as a witness, after considering such factors as (1) the child's age, (2) the child's cognitive and emotional development, (3) the child's need or desire to testify, (4) the

likelihood of emotional trauma or repercussions to the child, (5) the necessity of for the child's direct testimony, and (6) the availability of other evidence, hearsay exceptions, proffers, or stipulations that can substitute for direct testimony; and

h. if the child will be called as a witness, the setting of the child's testimony; for example, whether the child should testify in open court, open chambers, closed chambers, or another location.

Guideline C3. Ancillary Contact with the Child

The attorney should have meaningful contact with the child at least every six months, even if a court hearing is not scheduled. The attorney should seek to obtain notice of emergencies and significant events involving the child between court hearings. Upon receiving notice of such an event (for example, a change of placement), the attorney should interview or observe the child within a reasonable time. As necessary or appropriate to the representation, the attorney should attend treatment, placement, and administrative hearings, and other proceedings, as well as school case conferences or staffing conferences concerning the child.

Guideline C4. Continuity of Representation

The attorney should continue to represent the child after the initial court proceeding, including at disposition review hearings, permanency planning hearings, and related TPR and adoption proceedings.

D. ATTORNEY INVESTIGATION

Guideline D1. Independent Investigation

The child's attorney should conduct a thorough and independent investigation as necessary or appropriate to the representation. This investigation may include the following:

a. obtaining and reviewing the child's social services, psychiatric, psychological, drug and alcohol, medical, law enforcement, school, and other records relevant to the case;

b. interviewing or observing the child before all court hearings and when apprised of emergencies or significant events affecting the child;

c. interviewing school personnel and other professionals and potential witnesses;
d. interviewing the child's caretaker(s), with the permission of their attorney when necessary, concerning the type of services the child currently receives and the type of services the child needs; and
e. reviewing all relevant evidence.

At each stage of the investigation, the attorney should be familiar with the child's position

Guideline D2. Non-Verbal Child Without Considered Judgment

For a non-verbal child who does not have considered judgment, the attorney should observe that child in the child's environment and conduct a thorough investigation. The investigation should include, at a minimum, contact with the child's caretaker, teacher, physician, and caseworker to obtain information about the status of the child.

E. INVOLVEMENT IN THE COURT PROCESS

Guideline E1. Pre-Trial Stages

a. If the child has considered judgment, the attorney should develop a position and strategy concerning every relevant aspect of the proceedings. When developing the child's legal position, the attorney should ensure that the child is given advice and guidance and all information necessary to make an informed decision.
b. The attorney should explain to the child in a manner appropriate to the child's level of development what is expected to happen before, during, and after each hearing.
c. Consistent with the child's wishes, or the best interests of a child without considered judgment, the attorney should seek to obtain appropriate services, including services for children with physical, mental, or developmental disabilities.

Guideline E2. Trial Stages

a. The attorney should attend all hearings involving the child and participate in all telephone or other conferences with the court unless a particular hearing involves only issues completely unrelated to the child.

b. The attorney should present a case and make appropriate motions, including, when appropriate, introducing independent evidence and witnesses and cross-examining witnesses.

c. During all hearings, the attorney should preserve legal issues for appeal, as appropriate.

d. Consistent with the wishes of a child with considered judgment, the attorney should try to ensure timely hearings and oppose unwarranted continuances or postponements.

Guideline E3. Post-Trial Stages

a. Following the hearing, if consistent with the attorney's representation of the child's position, the attorney should seek a written court order to be given to the parties, containing at a minimum:
   (1) required findings of fact and conclusions of law;
   (2) the date and time of the next hearing;
   (3) required notices;
   (4) actions to be taken by each party, including the agency(ies), and custodians;
   (5) appropriate statutory timelines; and
   (6) the names of the parties who were present at the hearing.

b. The attorney should consider and discuss with the child the possibility and ramifications of an appeal and, when appropriate, take all steps necessary to note an appeal or participate in an appeal filed by another party.

F. ATTORNEY TRAINING

Guideline F1. Initial Training or Experience

Before accepting a case, an attorney who does not have sufficient experience in providing legal representation to children in CINA and related TPR and adoption cases should participate in formal training and education related to this area of practice. The attorney should satisfy the court and, if applicable, the entity responsible for payment of the attorney that the attorney has sufficient skill and experience in child advocacy. The attorney should participate in available training and education, including in-house training.

Guideline F2. Substance Of Training

Attorneys who seek to represent children in these proceedings are encouraged to seek training and education in such subjects as:

a. the role of child's attorney;
b. assessing considered judgment;
c. basic interviewing techniques;
d. child development: cognitive, emotional, and mental stages;
e. federal and state statutes, regulations, rules, and case law;
f. overview of the court process and key personnel in child-related litigation;
g. applicable guidelines and standards of representation;
h. family dynamics and dysfunction, including substance abuse and mental illness;
i. related issues, such as domestic violence, special education, mental health, developmental disability systems, and adult guardianships;
j. social service agencies, child welfare programs, and medical, educational, and mental health resources for the child and family; and
k. written materials, including related motions, court orders, pleadings, and training manuals.

G. ROLE OF THE COURT

If the court becomes aware that an attorney is not following these Guidelines, the court may encourage compliance by taking one or more of the following steps, as appropriate:

(1) alert the individual attorney that the attorney is not in compliance with the Guidelines;

(2) alert relevant government agencies or firms that the attorney is not complying with the Guidelines;

(3) alert the entity(ies) responsible for administering the contracts for children's representation that the attorney appointed to represent children is not complying with the Guidelines; and

(4) appoint another attorney for the child.

MARYLAND GUIDELINES FOR PRACTICE FOR COURT-APPOINTED ATTORNEYS REPRESENTING CHILDREN IN CASES INVOLVING CHILD CUSTODY OR CHILD ACCESS

Introduction and Scope

These Guidelines are intended to promote good practice and consistency in the appointment and performance of attorneys for children in cases involving child custody and child access decisions. However, the failure to follow a Guideline does not itself give rise to a cause of action against an attorney nor does it create any presumption that a legal duty has been breached. These Guidelines apply to divorce, custody, visitation, domestic violence, and other civil cases where the court may be called upon to decide issues relating to child custody or access. Nothing contained in the Guidelines is intended to modify, amend, or alter the fiduciary duty that an attorney owes to a client pursuant to the Maryland Attorneys' Rules of Professional Conduct.

These Guidelines do not apply to Child In Need of Assistance ("CINA"), Termination of Parental Rights ("TPR"), or adoption cases. The appointment and performance of attorneys appointed to represent children in those cases is addressed by the Guidelines of Advocacy for Attorneys Representing Children in CINA and Related TPR and Adoption Proceedings.

1. DEFINITIONS

A court that appoints an attorney for a minor child in a case involving child custody or child access issues should clearly indicate in the appointment order, and in all communications with the attorney, the parties, and other attorneys, the role expected of child's attorney. The terminology and roles used should be in accordance with the definitions in Guidelines 1.1–1.3.

1.1. Child's Best Interest Attorney

"Child's Best Interest Attorney" means an attorney appointed by a court for the purpose of protecting a child's best interest, without being bound by the child's directives or objectives. This term replaces the term "guardian ad litem." The Child's Best Interest Attorney makes an independent assessment of what is in the child's best interest and advocates for that before the court, even if it requires the disclosure of confidential information. The best interest attorney should ensure that the child's position is made a part of the record whether or not different from the position that the attorney advocates.

1.2. Child's Advocate Attorney

"Child's Advocate Attorney" means an attorney appointed by a court to provide an independent attorney for a child. This term replaces the less specific phrase, "child's attorney." A Child's Advocate Attorney owes the child the same duties of undivided loyalty, confidentiality, and competent representation as are due an adult client. A Child's Advocate Attorney should be appointed when the child is need of a voice in court, such as in relocation cases, when there are allegations of child abuse, or where the child is sufficiently mature and sees his or her interests as distinct from the interests of the child's parents.

1.3. Child's Privilege Attorney

"Child's Privilege Attorney" means an attorney appointed by a court in a case involving child custody or child access to decide whether to assert or waive, on behalf of a minor child, any privilege that the child if an adult would be entitled to assert or waive. This term replaces the term "Nagle v. Hooks Attorney." (*Nagle v. Hooks*, 296 Md. 123 (1983)). The court may combine the roles of Child's Privilege Attorney with either of the other two roles.

2. RESPONSIBILITIES

2.1 Determining considered judgment

The attorney should determine whether the child has considered judgment. To determine whether the child has considered judgment, the attorney should focus on the child's decision-making process, rather than the child's decision. The attorney should determine whether the child can understand the risks and benefits of the child's legal position and whether the child can reasonably communicate the child's wishes. The attorney should consider the following factors when determining whether the child has considered judgment:

(1) the child's developmental stage:
  (a) cognitive ability,
  (b) socialization, and
  (c) emotional and mental development;
(2) the child's expression of a relevant position:
  (a) ability to communicate with the attorney, and
  (b) ability to articulate reasons for the legal position; and
(3) relevant and available reports, such as reports from social workers, psychiatrists, psychologists, and schools.

A child may be capable of considered judgment even though the child has a significant cognitive or emotional disability. In determining whether a child has considered judgment, the attorney may seek guidance from professionals, family members, school officials, and other concerned persons. The attorney also should determine whether any evaluations are needed and request them when appropriate.

An attorney should be sensitive to cultural, racial, ethnic, or economic differences between the attorney and the child.

2.2 Child's Best Interest Attorney

A Child's Best Interest Attorney advances a position that the attorney believes is in the child's best interest. Even if the attorney advocates a position different from the child's wishes, the attorney should ensure that the child's position is made a part of the record. A Child's Best Interest Attorney may perform the following duties in fulfilling the attorney's obligation to the client and the court, as appropriate:

(a) Meet with and interview the child, and advise the child of the scope of the representation.
(b) Investigate the relative abilities of the parties in their roles as parents or custodians.

(c) Visit the child in each home.

(d) Conduct individual interviews with parents, and other parties, and witnesses.

(e) Observe the child's interactions with each parent and each other party, individually.

(f) Review educational, medical, dental, psychiatric, psychological, or other records.

(g) Interview school personnel, childcare providers, healthcare providers, and mental health professionals involved with the child or family.

(h) File and respond to pleadings and motions.

(i) Participate in discovery.

(j) Participate in settlement negotiations.

(k) Participate in the trial, including calling witnesses and presenting evidence and argument, as appropriate.

(l) If the child is to meet with the judge or testify, prepare the child, familiarizing the child with the places, people, procedures, and questioning that the child will be exposed to, and seek to minimize any harm to the child from the process.

(m) Inform the child in a developmentally appropriate manner when the representation is ending. A Child's Best Interest Attorney shall not testify at trial or file a report with the court.

2.3 Child's Advocate Attorney

If a Child's Advocate Attorney determines that the child has considered judgment, the attorney advances the child's wishes and desires in the pending matter. If a Child's Advocate Attorney determines that the child does not have considered judgment, the Child's Advocate Attorney should petition the court to (1) alter the attorney's role to permit the attorney to serve as a Child's Best Interest Attorney or (2) appoint a separate Child's Best Interest Attorney. A Child's Advocate Attorney may perform the following duties in fulfilling the attorney's obligation to the child and the court, as appropriate:

(a) Meet with and interview the child, and advise the child of the scope of the representation.

(b) Investigate the relative abilities of the parties in their role as parents or custodians.

(c) Visit the child in each home.

(d) Conduct individual interviews with parents, other parties, and collateral witnesses.

(e) Observe the child's interactions with each parent and each other party, individually.

(f) Review educational, medical, dental, psychiatric, psychological, or other records.

(g) Interview school personnel, childcare providers, healthcare providers, and mental health professionals involved with the child or family.

(h) File and respond to pleadings and motions.

(i) Participate in discovery.

(j) Participate in settlement negotiations.

(k) Participate in the trial, including calling witnesses and presenting evidence and argument, as appropriate.

(l) If the child is to meet with the judge or testify, prepare the child, familiarizing the child with the places, people, procedures, and questioning that the child will be exposed to, and seek to minimize any harm to the child from the process.

(m) Inform the child in a developmentally appropriate manner when the representation ends.

A Child's Advocate Attorney shall not testify at trial or file a report with the court.

2.4 Child's Privilege Attorney

A Child's Privilege Attorney notifies the court and the parties of the attorney's decision to waive or assert the child's privilege by (1) filing a document with the court prior to the hearing or trial at which the privilege is to be asserted or waived or (2) placing the waiver or assertion of privilege on the record at a pretrial proceeding or the trial.

A Child's Privilege Attorney may perform the following duties in fulfilling the attorney's obligation to the child and the court, as appropriate:

(a) Meet with and interview the child, and advise the child of the scope of the representation.
(b) Interview any witnesses necessary to assist the attorney in determining whether to assert or waive the privilege.
(c) Review educational, medical, dental, psychiatric, psychological, or other records.

3. CONFLICTS OF INTEREST

An attorney who has been appointed to represent two or more children should remain alert to the possibility of a conflict that could require the attorney to decline representation or withdraw from representing all of the children.

If a conflict of interest develops, the attorney should bring the conflict to the attention of the court as soon as possible, in a manner that does not compromise either client's interests.

4. TRAINING AND CONTINUING EDUCATION

Unless waived by the court, an attorney appointed as a Child's Best Interest Attorney, Child's Advocate Attorney, or Child's Privilege Attorney should have completed at least six hours of training that includes the following topics:

(a) applicable representation guidelines and standards;
(b) children's development, needs, and abilities at different stages;
(c) effectively communicating with children;
(d) preparing and presenting a child's viewpoint, including child testimony and alternatives to direct testimony;
(e) recognizing, evaluating, and understanding evidence of child abuse and neglect;
(f) family dynamics and dysfunction, domestic violence, and substance abuse;
(g) recognizing the limitations of attorney expertise and the need for other professional expertise, which may include professionals who can provide information on evaluation, consultation, and testimony on mental health, substance abuse, education, special needs, or other issues; and

(h) available resources for children and families in child custody and child access disputes.

Each court should require attorneys seeking appointments as a child's attorney to maintain their knowledge of current law and complete a specific amount of additional training over a defined interval.

5. QUALIFICATIONS

An attorney appointed to serve as a Child's Best Interest Attorney, Child's Advocate Attorney, or Child's Privilege Attorney should, as a minimum:

(a) be a member of the Maryland Bar in good standing, with experience in family law, or have been approved to represent children through a pro bono program approved by the bench; and

(b) unless waived by the court, have successfully completed the six hours of training specified in Guideline 4.

In addition, courts should seek to appoint attorneys who:

(a) are willing to take at least one pro bono appointment as a child's attorney per year, and

(b) have at least three years of family law experience or other relevant experience. In evaluating relevant experience, the court may consider the attorney's experience in social work, education, child development, mental health, healthcare, or other related fields.

6. COMPENSATION

6.1 Compensation structure

Each court should develop a compensation structure for the three roles of a child's attorney: Child's Best Interest Attorneys, Child's Advocate Attorneys, and Child's Privilege Attorneys.

6.2 Compensation mechanism

Each court should take steps to ensure that a child's attorney is compensated adequately and in a timely fashion, unless the attorney has been asked to serve pro bono publico. Courts may use the following mechanisms to ensure attorney compensation:

(a) Require one or more of the parties to deposit a significant retainer amount or a fixed fee determined by the court into an attorney escrow account or the court's registry.

(b) If a party qualifies for a fee waiver, compensate a child's attorney out of available funds. See Guideline 6.3.

(c) Enter a judgment for any unpaid fees.

6.3 Fee waivers

Each court should prepare its budget to ensure that it has sufficient funds to cover the expense of attorneys' fees for children when the parties are not able to pay the full fees, or the court should develop a pro bono publico component to its program to provide attorneys for children. Each court should apply the same fee waiver procedure, forms, and standard for the appointment of an attorney for a child that are set forth in the Guidelines for Grant Recipients for all family services funded by the Family Division/Family Services Program Grants. If a fee waiver is granted, the court should apply a cap on compensation that is appropriate to the role for which a child's attorney is appointed.

www.ingramcontent.com/pod-product-compliance
Ingram Content Group UK Ltd.
Pitfield, Milton Keynes, MK11 3LW, UK
UKHW020117290926
15471UKWH00003B/188

9 781960 444431